The Folio Book
of Literary Puzzles

JOHN SUTHERLAND

The Folio Book
of Literary Puzzles

London
The Folio Society
2007

'What Is the Professor's "Stuff"?', 'Who Moved Molly's Piano?', 'Who Killed Owen Taylor?' and 'Where Was Rebecca Shot?' are all from *Where Was Rebecca Shot?*, first published in Britain by Weidenfeld & Nicolson in 1998. The remaining essays are from *The Literary Detective: 100 Puzzles in Classic Fiction*, first published in Britain by Oxford University Press in 2000. This edition follows the text of those two editions with minor emendations. There are an additional two essays, exclusive to this edition, '*The Great Gatsby*, and the Chameleon on Wheels', and 'Brideshead: The Tradesman's Entrance'.

This edition is published by arrangement with The Orion Publishing Group Ltd and Oxford University Press

Frontispiece: *I Had Been There Before*. Illustration by Leonard Rosoman (© Leonard Rosoman 1995). From *Brideshead Revisited* by Evelyn Waugh, The Folio Society 1995.

PRINTED AND BOUND BY GRAFOS S.A., BARCELONA. BINDING ILLUSTRATION BY PETER SUART.

· CONTENTS ·

Previously Unpublished

· ILLUSTRATIONS ·

All illustrations are taken from Folio Society Publications.

· INTRODUCTION ·

Since the little puzzle amuses the ladies, it would be
a pity to spoil their sport by giving them the key.

*[Charlotte Brontë, concerning two female correspondents
who had written to her publisher enquiring about
the fate of Paul Emanuel in* Villette]

The chapters that follow are, in Miss Brontë's phrase, 'keys'.
Like those the young heroine comes across in *Alice in Wonderland* (which, as will be seen, has its little puzzle here) the
keys will not necessarily fit, although some turn better in
the narrative lock than others. No omniscience is claimed:
merely some speculative fun. The kind of fun, I believe, which
book-lovers like to indulge in as a tribute to the infinitely
fascinating appeal of the books they most love.

Great literature has always seemed to me to have that
quality which Matthew Arnold ascribes to the greatest of our
writers, Shakespeare:

> Others abide our question. Thou art free.
> We ask and ask: Thou smilest and art still,
> Out-topping knowledge.

'Ask and ask' could be the epigraph to this collection. The
texts, I hope, smile good-naturedly under the interrogation.
And, like Charlotte Brontë, they do not spoil the sport by
giving definitive answers.

Fun and literary criticism are not duck and green peas,
natural partners. The puzzles that follow have been gathered
from a series of light-hearted essays which I began publishing,
in book form in 1999, with *Is Heathcliff a Murderer?* ('Yes,'
I maintain – but not with entire confidence on the matter).

Pleasingly, that volume made it, for one glorious week, onto the *Sunday Times* best-seller list – not normally a place where academic criticism of Victorian fiction is to be found (although, when an Andrew Davies TV adaptation is running, Victorian fiction itself is often found there; *Middlemarch* actually topped the paperback best-seller list in March 1994). To be honest I think my fruit-fly moment of bestsellerdom may have spun off from Cliff Richard's musical, *Heathcliff*, which was running in the West End that season. But I am happy to share my glory with Sir Cliff. I went on to write five sequels, a selection from which (tied into Folio Society titles) is offered here.

The basis of these puzzles, as with other of the fundamental questions in our relationship with literature, is paradox. How is it that fiction – self-confessed falsehood – can be, in its strange way, so 'true'? By what processes can we be 'transported' into other worlds by a few black marks on a white surface? For all the wisdom of the academies (which get more wise on the subject, and less comprehensible, with every passing year) the childish explanation 'magic' suits as well as any.

It is not just readers who fall into the blur between reality and illusion. What did Trollope, for example, mean when he asserted, in *An Autobiography*, that 'his' characters were more real to him than the real people he passed in the streets of London? Coleridge's much used 'willing suspension of disbelief' does not quite cover what goes on between us and the novel – suggesting, as it does, a controlled response: a technique which we can turn on and off like a fire hose. The power of fiction over me, at least, has always been something that, try as I will, I cannot control. It, in a sense, controls (or takes over) me.

I will give a painful example: one in which there is no fun. Thackeray has always been my first love in Victorian fiction. It was with eagerness I went to see the 1975 Stanley Kubrick adaptation of *Barry Lyndon*. I was in the company of one of my PhD students – a woman working on Ouida (a writer who had become *her* first love in Victorian fiction). She was dying of cancer. Kubrick's film is, I think, superb. Particularly effective is the scene in which little Bryan is dying, having fallen off the horse his doting father has given him. The Victorians were good on deathbed moments (as good as contemporary novelists are on that other big thing that happens in bed). Kubrick played it for maximum pathos.

I confess that in the cinema that evening, my eyes moistened and I blubbed. And then caught myself up. What right had I to indulge myself by weeping at a false image, projected at ten frames a second onto a blank white screen, with a real, suffering person alongside me? When I mourned for her (as, alas, I would in a few months' time), would those tears be somehow more 'felt' than those spilled for the fictional film?

I can't answer the uncomfortable questions raised by such moments. What I will argue is that sometimes the primitive, self-surrendering attitude to fiction can yield, if not 'correct', then pleasurable and thought-provoking – if perverse – results.

I'll illustrate it again from personal experience. My teaching career over the last quarter-century has been conducted in two prestigious but very different institutions. In the UK, University College London has an English Department invariably ranked at the top of the league tables which are all the educational rage with Whitehall. It recruits very clever, very well read and critically sophisticated students. They know the ropes.

The other institution in which my split career has been conducted is the California Institute of Technology – probably the top-rated scientific institution in the world. Broad-based as American higher education is, even clever scientists have to take some 'humanities' requisites (along with Physical Education) to graduate. Hence me.

Although near genius in their specialist subjects, many Caltech students have little prior acquaintance with literary texts, or approved ways of reading them. The ropes are very strange to them. The consequences are often fascinating. On one course, examining popular fiction of the 1970s, one 'Techer', on being asked his verdict on Frederick Forsyth's *The Day of the Jackal,* responded, bluntly, 'It don't work.' On being asked why, he pointed to Chapter 14, where the hero 'solders' the ingenious firearm with which he intends to assassinate De Gaulle to the chassis of his car. 'The solder wouldn't hold,' the student went on to explain, with a welter of metallurgical detail. The gun would simply drop off. Hence, for that scientific literalist, nothing worked in the novel. It was not fiction, but busted fiction.

John Steinbeck's *The Grapes of Wrath* ends with one of the more famous scenes in American literature. Sheltering from the pitiless storm, the remnants of the shattered Joad family find themselves in a barn, with a starving man. They have no food, but the daughter, Rose of Sharon (deserted by her husband) is lactating, having just lost her baby:

> For a minute Rose of Sharon sat still in the whispering barn. Then she hoisted her tired body up and drew the comforter about her. She moved slowly to the corner and stood looking down at the wasted face, into the wide, frightened eyes. Then slowly she lay down beside him. He shook his head slowly from side to side. Rose of Sharon loosened one side of the blanket and bared her breast. 'You got to,' she said. She squirmed closer and pulled his head close. 'There!' she said. 'There.' Her hand moved behind his head and supported it. Her fingers moved gently in his hair. She looked up and across the barn, and her lips came together and smiled mysteriously.

Most readers, in my experience, read that last moment symbolically – only the poor can give sustenance for the poor. Dives will never help Lazarus. One of my Caltech students, however, set off on a methodical investigation of the nutritive value of human milk and how long, precisely, one suckle would maintain a fully grown man, on the verge of death. The result of the research was not reassuring. Rose of Sharon had nothing to smile about.

On yet another seminar occasion I provoked an intellectual riot by enquiring: 'If Vlad the Impaler vampirised his first victim, in the year of his death, 1476; and he and each of his subsequent victims vampirised one victim a year thereafter; how many of the un-Dead would there be, haunting the world, in 1896 – the year of *Dracula*'s action?' The answers, worked out to single-digit accuracy, demonstrated, conclusively, that (like Forsyth) Bram Stoker's novel 'don't work'. Another busted fiction.

It's nonsense, of course. The novels manifestly do work, otherwise they would not have lasted as triumphantly as they have to be mulled over by student literalists. But it is, none the less, fun sometimes to read novels 'primitively' as well as with the arsenal of critical weaponry which scholarship has burdened us with. To read them, that is, as 'real'. To impose, rather than suspend, disbelief. Which, modestly, the following chapters aim to do.

There is no need to recommend to members of the Folio Society the novels (overwhelmingly Victorian) from which these puzzles are taken. These essays on titles handsomely available in the Society's magnificent list are offered in a spirit of readerly fraternity and with the belief that there is more than one way to enjoy a good novel.

Postscript: with reference to Charlotte Brontë's puzzle, Paul Emanuel, I fear, will not return to his Lucy. But who, finally, can say?

JOHN SUTHERLAND
2007

What Is the Professor's 'Stuff'?

If there is one essential critical text for the understanding of
The Secret Agent it is Norman Sherry's *Conrad's Western
World*.[1] By resourceful sleuthing Sherry – over twelve chapters
– uncovers the 'originals' which inspired the novelist's 'Simple
Tale'. In one small detail, however, Sherry's explications may
mislead us. He assumes (as do most other commentators) that
the 'stuff' which the Professor gives Verloc, wherewith to
mount his explosive outrage on the first meridian, is dynamite.

Dynamite is, paradoxically, a 'safe' explosive, and one whose
useful applications (in mining, construction, and demolition)
have far outweighed its criminal misuses. Developed and
patented by Alfred Nobel (who magnanimously diverted a
portion of his ensuing profits to his 'Prizes'), dynamite represented a commercially viable way of stabilising the fearsomely
volatile liquid TNT (tri-nitro-toluene), by mixing it with a
suitably inert and solid base. Nobel's first successful compound
used *Kieselguhr* – a clayey substance. The resulting 'stick',
wrapped in waterproof cartridge paper, could be detonated
only by a smaller, controlled explosion in the form of a per-
cussion cap, an ignition fuse, or an electrical wire attached to
a plunger. The beauty of dynamite was that it could be safely
knocked, dropped, kicked or pounded without risk. You could
fall over carrying a hundredweight of the explosive, and suffer
nothing more than a sprained wrist. It was marketed as
'Nobel's safety powder'. TNT was something else. An unlucky
sneeze might detonate it.

Nobel's (trademarked) name for his product was an inspiration. Of all the names for explosives (cordite, gelignite, sem-
tex, C.4) it is the most resonantly poetic and memorable. In

the early 1880s 'dynamite' was quickly adapted into common currency as shorthand for any bomb-maker's gear. Revolutionaries became *dynamitards* – even though cartoonists would forever show them throwing the traditional black metal ball with the short fizzing fuse sticking out at the top.

In *The Secret Agent*, the word dynamite is used loosely on three occasions. 'A dynamite outrage must be provoked', Mr Vladimir tells the appalled Verloc, as he outlines the new regime under which the secret agent is to operate. A little later, Comrade Ossipon is described as a 'moribund veteran of the dynamite wars'. And as the Greenwich outrage reverberates through the corridors of power the 'great personage' (the Home Secretary, we apprehend) asks impatiently 'if this is the beginning of another dynamite campaign' (he is thinking presumably of recent Fenian outrages).

In fact, it is clear that the Professor's 'stuff' – whatever it may be – is *not* dynamite (a commodity which it would have been much easier to acquire from a mining contractor, or a quarry stockroom, than a crazy anarchist chemist). As Conrad recalls in his 1920 'Author's Note', the central episode of *The Secret Agent* was based on 'the already old [in 1907] story of the attempt to blow up the Greenwich Observatory; a blood-stained inanity of so fatuous a kind that it was impossible to fathom its origin'.

On 15 February 1894 Marcel Bourdin, a French anarchist, had prematurely detonated a bomb in Greenwich Park. Luckily he damaged only himself and some nearby trees. It was never established what his actual target was, nor how he intended to give himself time to escape (assuming that it was not a suicide mission). He survived the explosion – being able to whisper (in English, with a heavy French accent), 'take me home.' But his hand was blown off, and he died thirty minutes later in hospital of horrific fragment wounds to his abdomen.

Bourdin's device was described in *The Times*, 16 February, as 'a bottle which had apparently contained an explosive mixture'. This explosive mixture – whose 'character' was initially mysterious to the authorities – was (accidentally) detonated. Fragments of glass were found in the vicinity, together with Bourdin's missing body parts. It was supposed Bourdin had stumbled – possibly on a tree-stump – and the concussion prematurely detonated his bomb.

On 17 February, it was reported that there was new evidence as to the construction of the bomb in the shape of 'an all-important piece of iron, with five parallel grooves upon the inner side'. The metal fragment had been extracted from the wound in Bourdin's stomach. Its shape suggested 'the lip of a stone bottle' (or a metal container), about the 'size of a penny piece'. This piece of metal clearly worked against the 'glass bomb' hypothesis. And *The Times* was perplexed by the grooves in the iron fragment – 'perfect circles' not 'spiral' in form. They could not be a screw top, and – plausibly – had something to do with the timing device. By 19 February, the paper's special correspondent felt on safer ground with the explosive, reporting confidently that 'the bomb was charged with picric acid . . . a remarkably powerful explosive'. The paper continued: 'any person with a small knowledge of chemistry can make an engine of destruction out of a sardine box or an old saucepan' – but, it warned, 'expert assistance' would be required for the detonator and timing mechanism.

Bourdin's bomb was clearly not dynamite based. Nor, powerful as picric acid is, was it anywhere near as powerful a charge as that which disintegrates Stevie who (having 'stumbled', as it is supposed, 'against the root of a tree') is 'blown to small bits: limbs, gravel, clothing, bones, splinters – all mixed up together'. As Inspector Heat recalls with gratuitous relish, 'They had to fetch a shovel to gather him up with.' Most of Bourdin was intact.

Picric acid was an explosive favoured by the European military for artillery shells before the commercial availability of TNT. The disadvantage of picric acid and its derivatives was that they corroded metal containers (such as shell casings) and formed new, and unstable, chemical combinations. Hence the explosive needed to be kept in glass. If Bourdin's 'infernal machine' was picric-based, the combination of glass and metal fragments was logical. The circular grooves and the nature of the detonator remained mysterious.

It is clear from Conrad's narrative that, whatever explosive the Professor has secreted on his body, it is not dynamite, and may well be picric acid. He keeps it, as he tells Ossipon, 'in a thick glass flask'. When the time comes, it will be detonated with the same kind of pneumatic rubber ball used at the time in flash photography. There will be a twenty-second interval (the period marked in the studio by 'say cheese!'). Not one to hide his expertise in such matters (he was, after all, once a university lecturer), the Professor gives his anarchist colleagues a detailed description of the other 'infernal machine' he manufactured for Verloc:

'As he wanted something that could be carried openly in the hand, I proposed to make use of an old one-gallon copal varnish can I happened to have by me. He was pleased at the idea. It gave me some trouble, because I had to cut out the bottom first and solder it on again afterwards. When prepared for use, the can enclosed a wide-mouthed, well-corked jar of thick glass packed around with some wet clay, and containing sixteen ounces of X_2 green powder. The detonator was connected with the screw top of the can. It was ingenious – a combination of time and shock. I explained the system to him. It was a thin tube of tin, enclosing—.'

At this tantalising point, the Professor's exposition is interrupted, never to be resumed.

I do not know much about the home-manufacture of explosive devices, nor I think did Joseph Conrad. What he did was to throw together all the information he had gleaned from newspaper accounts of Bourdin's explosion. The 'sardine box'

becomes a one-gallon varnish can. The glass casing required for the brilliantly yellow liquid picric acid is retained. But, since the explosive is 'green powder' rather than yellow liquid, glass would seem superfluous. Nobel's *Kieselguhr* makes an entry as the wet clay packing – again superfluous; it would make more sense to surround the bomb with cotton wool or nails. The mysterious 'lip' extracted from Bourdin's stomach resurfaces as the varnish can's mouth. And what was the detonator on Stevie's bomb? We shall never know. But there may be a clue in the Professor's 'thin tube of tin'. Conrad, I suspect, had come across the following description of a time-delay detonator in the *Deutsches Offizierblatt*, 1906:

> In France an entirely different solution of the difficulties connected with the construction of long-range time fuses has been worked out. The time composition, which is a mixture of pulvérin and gum lac, is filled into a lead tube, which is then drawn out by passing through a number of draw plates until its diameter is reduced to a few millimetres. This tube, which burns very regularly, is wound in a spiral inside the fuse. To set the fuse, this tube is stabbed at the appropriate point, whereby the flame is caused to impinge on the priming at the proper time. The tube can, of course, be made of any desired length.[2]

The Professor's 'thin tube of tin' is a version of this French tubular timer. What one supposes is that: (1) screwing down the top of the can detonates a small cap which ignites the combustible substance compressed in the tube; (2) the contents of the tube are measured to burn for twenty minutes, before reaching the 'X2 powder'. The device needs careful handling since an unlucky jolt could forestall the whole process. As the Professor surmises, Stevie either screwed down the cap too early, or dropped the can.

It is clear that the Professor's device is based on Bourdin's tin-and-glass 'machine', with some Conradian refinements in the business of the detonator. It is clear, also, that the Professor's 'stuff' is the product of 'home industry' not Mr Nobel's Swedish factories. Is the Professor's 'stuff', then, 'stuff and nonsense'? Not quite. But neither is it an explosive device in the Freddy Forsyth class.[3]

Who Moved Molly's Piano?

A mischievously speculative article by Hugh Kenner in 1972 pointed to a teasing puzzle in *Ulysses*.[1] It pertains to what is, for Leopold Bloom, an overriding cause for anxiety on 16 June 1904: namely the affair between his wife Molly and the 'masher', Blazes Boylan. Their singing together, Bloom 'knows', is the pretext for his cuckolding. The scene in question occurs in the 'Ithaca' section – the pseudo-catechismic, question-and-answer description of Stephen and Leopold drinking tea, having returned late at night to the Bloom household. Stephen leaves and Leopold is suffused with sadness as he stands in the garden, having come outside to bid farewell to his young friend. He looks upwards at the stars:

Alone, what did Bloom feel?
  The cold of interstellar space, thousands of degrees below freezing point or the absolute zero of Fahrenheit, Centigrade or Réaumur: the incipient intimations of proximate dawn.

Having mournfully reviewed a roll-call of dead friends, as dawn breaks, Bloom returns into the house. He picks up a candle, and goes into the front room. He could, of course, find his way blindfold; he has done it so many times. But this occasion is painfully different:

What suddenly arrested his ingress?
  The right temporal lobe of the hollow sphere of his cranium came into contact with a solid timber angle where, an infinitesimal but sensible fraction of a second later, a painful sensation was located in consequence of antecedent sensations transmitted and registered.

This is to say, he bumps his head on the walnut sideboard. The front-room furniture has been moved during the day; the main change in the layout of the room is the piano over which Boylan and Molly hang during their musical rehearsals (in fact, rehearsals for more intimate duets). This instrument now occupies the position formerly occupied by the sideboard. Bloom, his head throbbing, contemplates the object at length:

> A vertical piano (Cadby) with exposed keyboard, its closed coffin supporting a pair of long yellow ladies' gloves and an emerald ashtray containing four consumed matches, a partly consumed cigarette and two discoloured ends of cigarettes, its musicrest supporting the music in the key of G natural for voice and piano of *Love's Old Sweet Song* (words by G. Clifton Bingham, composed by J. L. Molloy, sung by Madam Antoinette Sterling) open at the last page with the final indications *ad libitum, forte*, pedal, *animato*, sustained, pedal, *ritirando*, close.

We never know who moved the furniture, or why. The episode is, of course, a traditional joke which goes as far back as literature itself, about the philosopher, who while regarding the stars, falls into a pit. Leopold Bloom plays, momentarily, the absent-minded professor.

Who moved the piano? Bloom has been out of the house some five hours. It is unlikely that the Blooms' home help, the less than Amazonian Mrs Fleming, could have done it; at least by herself. And although Molly could have moved the chairs in the room, Kenner deduces that the piano and the sideboard would have been too much for her. Boylan must have done it. Kenner goes on to speculate why she would have had her lover do it. Because, he goes on to speculate, she wanted to avoid, postpone, or somehow sabotage the imminent sexual encounter with Blazes. The aim is to:

drain him . . . with exercise. She will postpone, perhaps evade, the physical moment; certainly reduce it. Across her mind, as they stand in the front room, flits her husband's frequent proposal to move that sofa to the ingleside. Masterstroke! She will wear Boylan down moving furniture, heavy furniture. And so, it seems, we are to imagine Blazes Boylan, redfaced, putting his shoulder to the sideboard, tugging at the piano, lifting and carrying the sofa and majolica-topped table, relocating the heavy chair, the light chair . . .

It's a nice scenario; and – if accepted – it subverts the erotic ruminations of Molly in 'Penelope'; we should see these not as factual, Kenner suggests, but as 'pornographic' fantasy. The reality of what went on between Mrs Bloom and her lover was very different.

Slight as the evidence is, Kenner's suggestion is material. It depends, pre-eminently, on one common-sense 'fact' – namely that moving pianos is no light task; not woman's work but man's labour. One thinks of that delicious Laurel and Hardy silent film in which the two clowns, with comically catastrophic results, attempt to move a piano up a flight of stairs.

Kenner's essay was amusingly controverted by a woman Joycean, Margaret Honton, in the *James Joyce Quarterly*, four years later. Citing quantities of chapter and verse (as Joyceans love to do in their internecine wars) Ms Honton's *coup de grâce* was her womanly familiarity (and, by implication, Kenner's male-chauvinist ignorance) of the realities of 'housework':

> I should like to persuade Mr Kenner and his readers of the likelihood of the women's [i.e. Molly and Mrs Fleming] moving the furniture by saying that I have moved an extremely heavy upright piano (Wegman) any number of times since I was twelve years old. A short distance, yes. Gradually, yes. And singly, yes. My experience with heavy Victorian furniture is that most of the pieces

are on castors, and some have handles – a sideboard would be a likely candidate for this – to facilitate moving. As for the bookcase, many a woman has moved larger cases than that by herself. One can take out the books first and replace them after the move, or venture to move the bookcase entire which usually necessitates picking up a few books scattered during the move.[2]

Professors, it would seem, are not just absent-minded; they also don't help much about the house.

Who Killed Owen Taylor?

Even by the standards of twist-a-minute hard-boiled detective fiction Raymond Chandler's plots are difficult to follow. Typically, to use his kind of simile, they have more holes than a Swiss cheese. The impenetrability of the plot of Chandler's first published novel, *The Big Sleep* (1938), gave rise to a famous literary anecdote.

The novel was filmed in 1946, by director Howard Hawks. This was the movie which 'made' the acting team, Bogart and Bacall. The couple fell in love during the shooting on the Warner lot, and married soon after. With *Casablanca*, *The Big Sleep* has become a classic of *film noir*. The image of 'Bogie' – fedora-hatted, smoking, above all *tough* – is a genre icon. As Chandler himself noted, for the rest of his career, Bogart retained 'something of Marlowe. He never lost it.'

During the shooting of the movie the director and his screenwriters (William Faulkner and Leigh Brackett) ran into an apparently insoluble turn of plot – who killed the Sternwoods' chauffeur, Owen Taylor? Hawks duly sent a telegram to Chandler, asking for guidance. Who was the guilty party? Back came the telegram, 'NO IDEA'. 'I never figured out what was going on,' Hawks later despairingly observed.[1] The 'No Idea' wire makes a good (and much repeated) story. But it is likely that Chandler was disinclined to help William Faulkner, of whom he may have been a little jealous. In fact the Owen Taylor sub-plot, although murky, suggests that the novelist had thought about it in some detail and worked out a range of possible developments.

When he arrives at the imposing Sternwood mansion, in the

upper Hollywood hills, Owen Taylor is the first person Philip Marlowe sees as he looks around the grounds:

> There were french doors at the back of the hall, beyond them a wide sweep of emerald grass to a white garage, in front of which a slim dark young chauffeur in shiny black leggings was dusting a maroon Packard convertible.

Both slim chauffeur and maroon Packard (Carmen Sternwood's vehicle, as we learn) will figure later.

The chauffeur (unnamed at this stage) reappears in the scene in which Geiger is taking his dirty pictures of a naked and drugged Carmen. Marlowe is keeping a gumshoe's watch on things from the dark street outside. After shots and a scream, Marlowe hears two cars speeding away. In the house he finds the naked Carmen and Geiger's corpse: a live nymphomaniac and a dead fag. Perfect. A studio camera has been set up. Clearly Geiger was planning to supplement his income as a high-class pornographer with some further lucrative blackmail of General Sternwood.

The photographic plate is missing from the camera. Who now has it? Marlowe tidies up as best he can (there is some collateral mystery about Geiger's corpse, which disappears and reappears), and deposits a blanketed and snoring Carmen back at the Sternwood residence.

The next morning, Marlowe is called by his pal in the District Attorney's department, Bernie Ohls. An automobile has been driven into the ocean at 'Lido Fish Pier' (San Pedro, apparently – the harbour thirty miles from downtown LA). There is a body. The dead man proves to be Owen Taylor, the Sternwoods' chauffeur. The automobile is the Buick sedan of the older Sternwood daughter, Vivian. The cause of Taylor's death is mysterious. He has a broken neck – which may or may not be a result of the impact of the car hitting the ocean. The detectives' trained eyes soon perceive, however, that he was

'sapped' with a blackjack at some point before his death.

Evidently the Buick crashed through the end-of-the-pier barrier at high speed – having been driven straight down the whole length of the structure. This, then, is no 'accident'. The 'hand throttle' (i.e. hand-operated accelerator – a device found on pre-war limousines, equivalent to today's 'cruise control') had been set halfway down. Unlike the foot-operated accelerator, this could have been done by someone other than the driver, who might then have thrown the car in gear and set it off, effectively driving itself, if the man at the wheel were unconscious. Taylor may well have been bumped off.

There is still no sign of the blackmail photo of Carmen in the altogether. If the dead man ever had it, he has it no longer. There are obvious mysteries here. The film chose to cut them short by making the Taylor crash manifestly accidental and wholly enigmatic. The death off the end of a fishing-pier left too many threads hanging for Howard Hawks to clear up in his scanty 118 minutes of screen time. Nor was Chandler inclined to be helpful. In the film, Taylor is now forgotten. The audience's attention is directed to other more profitable matters.

In the novel, with its more spacious dimensions, further teasing details about Taylor ooze out over the following chapters. Police investigation reveals that a year or two ago he was arrested on a 'Mann Act rap' – the federal 'white slavery' law which prohibits the transport of minors for sexual purposes across state lines. As Ohls explains:

'It seems Taylor run Sternwood's hotcha daughter, the young one [i.e. Carmen], off to Yuma. The sister [i.e. Vivian] ran after them and brought them back and had Owen heaved into the icebox. Then next day she comes down to the DA and gets him to beg the kid off with the US 'cutor. She says the kid meant to marry her sister . . . So we let the kid go and then darned if they don't have him come back to work. And a little later we get the routine report on his prints from Washington, and he's got a prior back in Indiana, attempted hold-up six years ago. He got off with a six months in the county jail, the very one Dillinger bust out of. We hand that to the Sternwoods and they keep him on just the same. What do you think of that?'

'They seem to be a screwy family,' Marlowe laconically replies. It later emerges that Carmen carries in her handbag a cute little pearl-handled .22 revolver, engraved 'CARMEN FROM OWEN' (this is the gun with which she has killed Rusty Regan, and will try to kill Marlowe).

What went on at Geiger's Hollywood bungalow, on the night of his murder, gradually emerges. Carmen was somehow enticed to the house. She was drugged on the premises with a mixture of ether and opium – taken 'for kicks' apparently. There is no need to slip this young lady anything. Carmen had driven herself to Geiger's place in her maroon Packard convertible, still gleaming presumably from the chauffeur's loving chamois.

Taylor, the same evening, had taken Vivian's car without permission. What was he doing in it? 'Nobody knows,' Vivian tells Marlowe. But we can make an educated guess. Geiger, having taken his photographs, would have needed someone to take the incapable young woman home. He, as prospective blackmailer, could hardly drop her off himself. So he phoned the chauffeur. Alternatively, Taylor was there all the time, and he was the bait that got Carmen to the house in the first place. It was their 'love nest', and had been used for such assignations before. This might also explain how it was Carmen came to be undressed. Failing some such explanation it is hard to see what Carmen was doing in Geiger's seedy joint and why a good-time girl like her would want to spend an evening there.

There was, however, another player in this game that no one knew about. In addition to Marlowe, Geiger was being tailed by Joe Brody. Brody's aim was to move in on Geiger's pornographic lending-library racket. Confronted later by a gun-wielding Marlowe, Brody insists, 'I *didn't* bop Geiger.' It was Taylor.

According to Brody, the chauffeur broke into Geiger's place 'to have words with him, because Owen Taylor was sweet on Carmen, and he didn't like the kind of games Geiger was playing with her'. When he saw the precise nature of the 'games' he lost his head and shot Geiger three times in the belly. If he was so 'sweet on Carmen' it would seem logical at this point for lover-boy to have taken her home, called the police, or at least covered the naked young lady up. Instead of which Taylor grabbed the photographic plate, leaving the nude Carmen for someone else to take care of. A strange kind of sweetheart, we may think.

Clutching the photographic plate Taylor shot off at speed in Vivian's car, hotly pursued by Brody (hence the two cars which Marlowe heard). In a sharp turn off Sunset Boulevard, Taylor (according to Brody) skidded off the road. Brody 'sapped' him with his blackjack while he was still dazed, and took the plate-holder 'just out of curiosity'. Why he should engage in a high-speed chase, simply in order to crack Taylor on the skull, and take nothing except an undeveloped negative of whose nature he is unaware, is another can of narrative worms.

The suggestion is that when he came round from being sapped, Taylor was so suffused with remorse that, having heaved his heavy sedan back on the road, he drove it thirty miles to the coast to drive it off the road again into the Pacific. He committed suicide by accelerating at top speed (using the 'hand accelerator') along the Lido Fish Pier. It might well be an unpleasant death (drowning in a slowly sinking car) and it is hard to imagine a young hardened criminal inflicting it on himself. Taylor still has a revolver with three bullets in it (he plugged Geiger with the other three). If, as seems wholly unlikely that he would, he had resolved to kill himself, why not just blow his head off? Most likely, of course, is that young Mr

Taylor would take off down the Pacific Coast Highway for Mexico, sell the car for as many pesos as he could get, and keep his head down until it was safe to come back.

This is how the narrative leaves things. Slightly farther along than Howard Hawks and William Faulkner do in the film, but still tantalisingly unexplained. The Los Angeles newspapers report Taylor's death as suicide, and Marlowe lets sleeping dogs lie – or this dog at least. According to the papers, 'Owen Taylor had been despondent and in poor health. His family lived in Dubuque, and his body would be shipped there. There would be no inquest.'

Who then killed Owen Taylor? Owen Taylor himself? The business about poor health and despondency is hogwash; chauffeurs can't afford such luxuries. How did the papers come by it? From someone in the Sternwood household, obviously. As chauffeur, Taylor would have had his own keys to the Buick, but it is hard to believe that he could have taken the pride of the Sternwood auto fleet without someone in the house knowing. Or without permission from the car's owner, Vivian (a ruthless woman). Who put the fix in at City Hall, and ensured there was no inquest? A Sternwood, obviously – the family has 'pull'.

Above all, why, after killing Geiger, did Taylor take the photographic plate? Not to protect Carmen, we deduce. It's easy to destroy undeveloped negatives – all you have to do is expose the sensitised surface to the light. Why, on his part, did Brody go to the trouble of chasing after Taylor, and – having caught him – take the plate 'just out of curiosity'? A curiosity which led to having the plate developed (privately, of course; you can't expect a main-street druggist to hand over pictures of a naked woman without some query).

One doesn't have to be Marlowe to work out a more likely scenario than suicide. Taylor, we may plausibly deduce, was blackmailing the Sternwoods. On that trip to Yuma, he got something on Carmen that made it impossible for the family to dismiss him (even though, as a convicted felon, he could not legally have a commercial driver's licence, let alone a permit for the gun he was carrying). He was a pain in the Sternwood neck, ripe for rubbing out. Vivian had a friend, Eddie Mars, who specialised in such favours.

Taylor was, meanwhile, in cahoots with Geiger – and quite possibly with Brody. He shot the fat pornographer, in order to get the negative, seeing the chance of a really big score from General Sternwood. Carmen was in no position to testify against him. He had too much on her. In all probability, Taylor was also hooked up with Brody. The two men arranged to double-cross Geiger. They met on Sunset Boulevard by arrangement (no skidding car). Brody then double-crossed Taylor, knocking him out (for the police to find and nail for the murder), and making off with the negatives.

What neither Taylor nor Brody knew was that Vivian had put a contract out on the chauffeur, with her pal Eddie Mars (Geiger's landlord, surprisingly enough). After Taylor was sapped and Brody had left the scene, one of Mars's heavies (Canino?) took the still-unconscious Taylor down to the coast in the Buick (followed by a henchman in a second car) and staged the 'suicide'. If anyone had been prepared to pay Marlowe $25 a day plus expenses, he would have uncovered it all. But Taylor didn't matter that much. He was expendable – a bit player, he's ultimately as forgettable as Howard Hawks makes him in the film.

The question of course is – did Chandler expect the canny reader to work this out for himself? Or did he leave it there, as a kind of reserve plot, to fall back on, should the denouement require it? Or is it there to generate an enveloping narrative fog – like the pea-soupers in the Sherlock Holmes films? One can't know. And if Chandler wouldn't confide in Hawks or Faulkner, we never shall know.

Where Was Rebecca Shot?

Daphne du Maurier's romance is replete with enigma and unanswered questions left hanging artfully over the plot and its cunning denouement. Four puzzles stand out: (1) What are the second Mrs de Winter's Christian and maiden names, and what is her background? (2) Whose is the body which, at Edgecoombe, Maxim de Winter identified, two months after her disappearance, as that of his wife? (knowing, all the while, that Rebecca's corpse is lying underwater in the cabin of *Je reviens,* a few hundred yards from the boathouse); (3) Why, in his last encounter with Rebecca, did Maxim fortuitously have a loaded gun with him? (4) If Mrs Danvers set fire to Manderley, Maxim's great house, what happened to her after this act of criminal arson?

The awkward anonymity and 'out-of-nowhere' character of the heroine-narrator of the story is not a puzzle which one would want solved. Her complete absence of history, past life or identity, her affectless character, create a vacuum to be filled with the unexpurgated presence of the dead-but-not-dead ('I shall return') Rebecca. In life the nameless one is less alive than dead Rebecca. The gimmick was respected by Hitchcock in his 1940 film (Joan Fontaine is listed as 'the girl') and by Susan Hill, in her authorised sequel, *Mrs de Winter* (1993).

Effective and novel-seeming as it is, one would like to know who first used the device of the omnipresent but nameless heroine-narrator, if not du Maurier. It seems to derive in part from the author's reading of Kafka. As with 'Josef K' in *The Trial,* it creates a striking vacuousness at the heart of the novel. In *Rebecca*'s case the effect is heightened by the narrative's being otherwise excessively and lushly descriptive. Du Maurier's 'no-name' trick is, one concludes, worth all the contortions which the dialogue has to perform to avoid accidentally dropping the girl's first name. But the fact that the main character was unnamed made it difficult to promote the film and Joan Fontaine's starring role. That Fontaine played 'Rebecca' has become one of popular culture's ubiquitous vulgar errors.

Hitchcock also had some difficulty with the other lady in the water.[1] Two months after Rebecca's disappearance – presumably at sea – a body was washed up 'Near Edgecoombe, about forty miles up channel' (the Bristol Channel, in the West Country). It is assumed by the authorities that she ('Rebecca') must have been drowned, 'trying to swim to shore after the boat sank'. The body was then taken by the tides on its long voyage up the tidal channel while undergoing its sea change.

Even the narrator-heroine, who is no yachtswoman, thinks this course of events is odd: 'I thought drowned people were found after two days. I thought they would be washed up close to the shore when the tide came.' Maxim went to court to identify the corpse and confirmed it was that of his wife. He must, one presumes, have knowingly falsified his sworn testimony, although it is not entirely beyond conceiving that he might have deluded himself that Rebecca's body had somehow drifted out of the closed cabin in which he left it, before scuttling the three-ton *Je reviens*. But perjury is the more likely hypothesis. It must have been touch-and-go: in the 1930s a lady like Mrs de Winter would surely have a wedding ring which must (mysteriously to the coroner's office) not have been on the corpse's left hand. If the body were so decomposed that the flesh on the fingers had sloughed off, by what means *did* Maxim identify it?

Some twelve months after this false identification, Rebecca's true body is found in the cabin of her yacht by divers investigating the wreck of another vessel gone down on the cove's treacherous rocks just a few hundred yards from Manderley. There are, even at this early stage, some mysteries which the

Edgecoombe coroner seems flagrantly to have neglected: why, for example, the substantial three-ton, wooden boat sank like a stone after capsizing without any wreckage being washed up on any shore. Did Maxim hint to the coroner that Rebecca had gone, solo, on a long voyage out to sea?

Another puzzle is why, when the real Rebecca's corpse is discovered, no one seems in the slightest curious as to who the other 'pseudo-Rebecca' can have been. The magistrate, Colonel Julyan, instigates the most vigorous (and patently corrupt) investigations into the second, actual Rebecca corpse – culminating in the astonishing interview with Dr Baker, the cover-up as to the circumstances of her death, and the discreet advice that the de Winters might find it convenient to spend a decade or two in Switzerland. But no one (least of all the Colonel) seems to think, even as a hypothesis, that the other woman may have been on the boat with Rebecca.

This hypothesis has a far-fetched plausibility. The first Mrs de Winter's lesbian tastes are clearly established. 'Rebecca was incapable of love, of tenderness, of decency,' Max bitterly recalls, 'she was not even *normal*' (my italics). Mrs Danvers is blunter: 'She despised all men. She was above all that.' The other woman's presence on the boat would explain how it might be that, at the time of the supposed capsize, Rebecca was below decks with the cabin door closed on her.

There is a second inquest for Rebecca, a second formal identification of the corpse by Maxim, and a second interment in the vault at Manderley. But there is no second inquest for the nameless pseudo-Rebecca. And where is her disinherited corpse laid to rest? In Potter's Field, presumably. Or perhaps it is tossed back into the waves whence it came.

A connected hypothesis invites passing examination. Did Maxim come on Rebecca *in flagrante delicto* with a *woman* in the boathouse, and kill them both, unable to restrain himself on witnessing, in its full 'unspeakability', the Sapphic depravity of his wife? Obviously he would not have been able to stow both corpses in the cabin and sustain the accidental capsize theory when the wreck was eventually discovered (as he must have known it would be). The other body may have been left on deck, or taken up the coast in his own yacht, and deposited miles away at sea.

This leads on to the third of the puzzles: why did Maxim take a gun with him when he went down to the boathouse for his last interview with Rebecca? And what kind of 'gun' (shotgun, rifle, or handgun) was it? His repeated mention that the single fatal 'bullet' went right through Rebecca, without scraping or smashing any bone, suggests either a rifle or a large-calibre handgun. Anatomically, the route which the fatal round must have taken is through the soft tissue of the belly or abdomen (more of which later). Although we have no firm information on the matter, Maxim presumably served in the Great War, and would be a trained shot; he would also know how best to kill your man. The heart, or head, would of course be the logical target; unless he had an ulterior motive in what marksmen call a 'gut-shot'. It's very nasty – more so since Maxim now 'knows' that his wife is carrying a baby. He is ending two lives. Hitchcock in his film blurred the whole thing by having Rebecca start back at the sight of Max's fury, fall over, bang her head, and die accidentally. No gut-shot, no blood.

Why was Maxim so enraged as to want to go rampaging down to the boathouse, gun in hand? He has no reason to suppose that Rebecca has a lover with her, after her return from London. As he tells his second wife: 'I came back after dinner, about half past ten, and I saw her scarf and gloves lying on a chair in the hall. I wondered what the devil she had come back for.' '*Her* scarf and gloves': no one else's. Maxim's explanation to his second wife for storming down to the boathouse, fully armed, rings very hollow. He claims to have suspected that she had a (male) lover with her, probably the obnoxious Jack Favell: 'The thing had got to be settled, one way or the other. I thought I'd take a gun and frighten the fellow, frighten them both.' If he just wants to 'frighten' them, why take a loaded weapon? He would, of course, have to insert the shells before rushing down to the boathouse; countrymen and ex-officers like Maxim do not leave loaded weapons round the house. It is part of the licence under which they hold them that they do not.

Maxim, as he recalls, found Rebecca alone, although it later emerges that she had left an urgent message at Jack Favell's flat, on leaving London a few hours previous. The message bears interestingly on Maxim's account (he does not know of its existence when he makes his confession to his second wife). 'I tried to ring you from the flat,' Rebecca writes to Jack:

> 'but could get no answer. I'm going down to Manders right away. I shall be at the cottage this evening, and if you get this in time will you get the car and follow me. I'll spend the night at the cottage, and leave the door open for you. I've got something to tell you and I want to see you as soon as possible. Rebecca.'

The 'something' she has to tell him, obviously, is that she has only months to live. Why tell Jack before anyone else? Because, as he apprehends ('This cancer business . . . does anybody know if it's contagious?'), the disease is venereal in origin. If she has it, so does he. Dr Baker of course is tactful on this aspect of Rebecca's disorder. Surprised by Maxim in the boathouse, according to his version of events, Rebecca taunted him with the 'news' that she is pregnant by another man. She will pass the child off as heir to Manderley. There are numerous hints in the narrative that theirs is a 'blank', unconsummated union ('Our marriage was a farce from the very first . . . We never loved each other, never had one moment of happiness together').

Rebecca knows that this malicious invention will madden Maxim and (again according to his account) she turns the screw ruthlessly on her husband:

'If I had a child, Max . . . neither you, nor anyone in the world, would ever prove that it was not yours. It would grow up here in Manderley, bearing your name. There would be nothing you could do. And when you died Manderley would be his. You could not prevent it. The property's entailed. You would like an heir, wouldn't you, for your beloved Manderley? . . . Well, you heard me say I was going to turn over a new leaf, didn't you? Now you know the reason . . . I'll be the perfect mother, Max, like I've been the perfect wife.'

It is all too much for the cuckolded Max:

'She turned round and faced me, smiling, one hand in her pocket, the other holding her cigarette. When I killed her she was smiling still. I fired at her heart. The bullet passed right through. She did not fall at once. She stood there, looking at me, that slow smile on her face, her eyes wide open . . . I'd forgotten', said Maxim, and his voice was slow now, tired, without expression, 'that when you shot a person there was so much blood.'

One notes, as a point of passing interest, that Maxim has clearly shot people before. And one notes how carefully he chooses his words: 'I fired *at* her heart.' He missed, of course. It is inconceivable that even a small-calibre bullet (a .22 round, say) could miss hitting a bone in the ribcage on entry or exit. And it would have to be a very powerful gun indeed for the bullet to pass through the whole width of the (presumably corseted) body, causing enough damage to vital organs to kill the victim with one wound. If the bullet had remained lodged in the body it would, of course, have been found by the post-mortem.

Maxim is a liar on oath: a proven perjurer. And there are aspects of this which ring false. He intends to straighten things out 'one way or another', but he takes a loaded gun only to 'frighten the fellow'. Or possibly to frighten Rebecca as well.

Why Rebecca should want to taunt him into killing her, before having had her little talk with Jack, is mysterious. As Maxim reconstructs the scene, it was she who was to blame. She manipulated him into pulling the trigger of the gun which, quite fortuitously, he happened to have with him. It is, of course, the classic (and often successful) defence of the wife-killer: 'She taunted me with my manhood, Your Honour; a red mist came over my eyes and I didn't know what I was doing.' Justifiable homicide; three years' probation.

Then there is the business of the single shot that killed Rebecca. If, as Maxim says, the bullet went through her body, killing her without touching a bone, we have to assume that he shot her in the belly, above the pelvis and below the ribs. He claims to have aimed at her false heart. But, since the heart is an organ encased by bone, he clearly either missed or is lying. What seems more plausible is that with her cigarette-holding hand Rebecca pointed to her stomach, the lodging-place for the embryonic heir of Manderley, and that is where Maxim shot her.

If we look through Maxim's terse, self-serving description to what more probably happened, it throws an unromantic light on the master of Manderley. Should we believe, in the first place, that he went down to the boathouse simply to put the frighteners on Rebecca and her lover? What seems plausible, given Max's explosive temper (of which we are given many examples), is that he apprehended, from the coat and scarf, that Rebecca was in the boathouse by herself, and went down intending to kill her. She pleaded for her life, claiming (falsely) that she was pregnant. It is the kind of ruse that would come naturally to her. Implacable, Maxim shot her in the stomach. With a great deal of cunning, it is possible for narrative to handle such scenes and retain some degree of sympathy for the murderer. I have witnessed an audience cheer, for example, at that last scene in the film *Fatal Attraction* where the pregnant *femme fatale* (played by Glenn Close) is shot in the stomach.

But it would be hard, if we had a more candid account than Maxim de Winter's own, to see what he did as anything other than cold-blooded, premeditated murder.

As to the fire at Manderley, both the Hitchcock film and the 1995 TV version made it a grand climax, a kind of lesbian suttee. Mrs Danvers is shown, inside the house, setting the fire (hard to do, one would have thought, with a household full of servants). Mrs Danvers then immolates herself in the flames, in the shrine of Rebecca's bedroom. The suggestion is that they were lovers (unappetising as 'Danny' is, physically). Susan Hill makes Mrs Danvers the arsonist, but has her survive to return and persecute the second Mrs de Winter, ten years later.

In the novel, the fire is more enigmatic. The de Winters arrive by car, at four o'clock in the morning. Maxim is apprehensive. He has been informed that Mrs Danvers had a trunk phone call, and has packed up and left. As they approach Manderley, the narrator-heroine sees, as she thinks, the dawn rising in the west. But it cannot be. Are they perhaps 'northern lights'? Not in summer:

> He drove faster, much faster. We topped the hill before us and saw Lanyon lying in a hollow at our feet. There to the left of us was the silver streak of the river, widening to the estuary at Kerrith six miles away. The road to Manderley lay ahead. There was no moon. The sky above our heads was inky black. But the sky on the horizon was not dark at all. It was shot with crimson, like a splash of blood. And the ashes blew towards us with the salt wind from the sea.

And so the novel ends. The questions remain. Who has done this vengeful act, set fire to Manderley? Rebecca, of course. *Je reviens.*

Apple-Blossom in June?

The early nineteenth-century novelists inherited from their Gothic predecessors a sense that, where landscape was concerned, lies were more beautiful than truth and, for that reason, often preferable. In his essay on Mrs Radcliffe in *The Lives of the Novelists*, Scott notes the pervasive vagueness of her scene-painting, a quality which at its best aligns her word-drawn settings with the imaginary landscapes of Claude:

> Some artists are distinguished by precision and correctness of outline, others by the force and vividness of their colouring; and it is to the latter class that this author belongs. The landscapes of Mrs Radcliffe are far from equal in accuracy and truth to those of her contemporary, Mrs Charlotte Smith, whose sketches are so very graphical, that an artist would find little difficulty in actually painting from them. Those of Mrs Radcliffe, on the contrary, while they would supply the most noble and vigorous ideas, for producing a general effect, would leave the task of tracing a distinct and accurate outline to the imagination of the painter. As her story is usually enveloped in mystery, so there is, as it were, a haze over her landscapes, softening indeed the whole, and adding interest and dignity to particular parts, and thereby producing every effect which the author desired, but without communicating any absolutely precise or individual image to the reader.[1]

For all the realism of his historical analysis and characterisation, Scott often found a similar 'haze' very useful in his own higher-flying landscape descriptions. It was pointed out to him when embarking on *Anne of Geierstein* (1829) that it might be a handicap never to have visited the Swiss Alps, where the

action is set. Nonsense, Scott replied, he had seen the paint-
ings of Salvator Rosa, and that would do very well, thank you.[2]
Radcliffian haze was also very useful to Scott in what remains
the most famous anomaly in his fiction, the 'reversed sunset'
in *The Antiquary* (1816). In an early big scene in that novel, Sir
Arthur Wardour and his daughter Isabella are trapped between
the onrushing tide and unscalable cliffs. The location is iden-
tifiably Newport-on-Tay (called in the novel 'Fairport'), near
Dundee, on the east coast of Scotland. Scott highlights the
scene by having it occur while the great disc of the sun sinks
into the North Sea – a lurid panorama on which two paragraphs of fine writing are lavished.

The problem is, of course, that in our cosmos the sun does
not sink in the east, it sinks in the west, in the Irish Sea.
Given the haste with which he wrote his novel it is not surprising,
perhaps, that Scott should have perpetrated the error. What is
surprising is that he should have retained it in his 1829 revised
edition of *The Antiquary*. The mistake was certainly pointed out
to him. Evidently he felt that where land and seascapes were
concerned, the novelist's artistic licence extended to changing
the course of the planets through the heavens. Novelists later
in the century were more fastidious. Rider Haggard, for instance,
rewrote large sections of *King Solomon's Mines* in order to correct an error about the eclipse of the sun which is so technical
as to be beyond all but the most astronomically expert readers. Haggard mistakenly had the solar eclipse occur while the
moon was full. In all editions of *King Solomon's Mines* after the
'37th thousand' he changed it to a lunar eclipse.

This fetishism about scenic detail develops in the 1830s and
1840s. It may well have coincided with more sophistication
about the authenticity of theatrical sets, a greater awareness of
what foreign parts looked like with the growth of the British
tourism industry, and the diffusion of encyclopaedias among
the novel-reading classes. Captain Frederick Marryat wrote
Masterman Ready, or the Wreck of the Pacific (1841) specifically

to correct the travesty of life on a South Seas desert island perpetrated by Johann Wyss's *The Swiss Family Robinson* (1812,
1826). Marryat, who as a sailor had felt the brine of the seven
seas on his cheek, was appalled by such freaks of nature as
flying penguins and man-eating boa-constrictors.

Jane Austen's most lamentable landscape-painting error occurs in the Donwell picnic scene in *Emma*. The date of the
picnic is given to us very precisely. 'It was now the middle of
June, and the weather fine,' we are told. And again, a few
pages later, the excursion is described as taking place 'under a
bright mid-day sun, at almost Midsummer' (i.e. around 21
June). Strawberries are in prospect, which confirms the June
date. During the course of the picnic, Austen indulges (un-
usually for her) in an extended passage describing a distant
view – specifically Abbey-Mill Farm, which lies some half a mile
distant, 'with meadows in front, and the river making a close
and handsome curve around it'. The narrative continues,
weaving the idyllic view into Emma's tireless matchmaking activities:

> It was a sweet view – sweet to the eye and the mind. English ver-
> dure, English culture, English comfort, seen under a sun bright,
> without being oppressive.
>
> In this walk Emma and Mr Weston found all the others as-
> sembled; and towards this view she immediately perceived Mr
> Knightley and Harriet distinct from the rest, quietly leading the
> way. Mr Knightley and Harriet! – It was an odd tête-à-tête; but
> she was glad to see it. – There had been a time when he would
> have scorned her as a companion, and turned from her with little
> ceremony. Now they seemed in pleasant conversation. There had
> been a time also when Emma would have been sorry to see Har-
> riet in a spot so favourable for the Abbey-Mill Farm; but now she
> feared it not. It might be safely viewed with all its appendages of
> prosperity and beauty, its rich pastures, spreading flocks, orchard
> in blossom, and light column of smoke ascending.

Terry Castle in the Oxford World's Classics edition offers a note to 'in blossom':

> The anomaly of an orchard blossoming in the strawberry season was noticed by some of the novel's first readers. Jane Austen's niece Caroline wrote to a friend as follows: 'There is a tradition in the family respecting the apple-blossom as seen from Donwell Abbey on the occasion of the strawberry party and it runs thus – That the first time my uncle . . . saw his sister after the publication of *Emma* he said, "Jane, I wish you would tell me where you get those apple-trees of yours that come into bloom in July." In truth she did make a mistake – there is no denying it – and she was speedily apprised of it by her brother – but I suppose it was not thought of sufficient consequence to call for correction in a later edition.'

One could defend the anachronistic apple-blossom in the same way that one defends the anastronomical sunset in that other novel of 1816, *The Antiquary*. Both represent a hangover from the free-and-easy ways of the Gothic novel of the 1790s when such liberties could be taken with artistic impunity. But this is not entirely satisfactory with the author of *Northanger Abbey*, a novel which hilariously castigates Gothic fiction's offences against common sense. And, as R. W. Chapman notes (apropos of the apple-blossom), such mistakes are 'very rare' in Miss Austen's fiction.[3]

It was evidently assumed by Jane Austen's family that no correction was made because the error was 'not thought of sufficient consequence'. This is unlikely; elsewhere one can find Jane Austen going to some length to authenticate detail in her fiction (she put herself to trouble, for instance, to verify details as to whether there was a governor's house in Gibraltar, for *Mansfield Park*).

If the 'apple-blossom in June' error was pointed out to her, why then did Jane Austen not change it? 'Orchards in leaf' would have been an economical means of doing so, requiring no major resetting of type. One explanation is that she did not have time – some eighteen months after the publication of *Emma* Jane Austen died, in July 1817. A more appealing explanation is that it is not an error at all. It was not changed because the author did not believe it was wrong. In order to make this second case one should note that there is not one 'error' in the description (blossom in June), but two, and possibly three. Surely, on a sweltering afternoon in June, there would not be smoke rising from the chimney of Abbey-Mill Farm? Why have a fire? And if one were needed for the baking of bread, or the heating of water in a copper for the weekly wash, the boiler would surely be lit before dawn, and extinguished by mid-morning, so as not to make the kitchen (which would also be the family's dining-room) unbearably hot. The reference to the ascending smoke would seem to be more appropriate to late autumn. And the reference to 'spreading flocks' would more plausibly refer to the lambing season, in early spring, when flocks enlarge dramatically. It will help at this point to quote the relevant part of the passage again: 'It might be safely viewed with all its appendages of prosperity and beauty, its rich pastures, spreading flocks, orchard in blossom, and light column of smoke ascending.' What this would seem to mean is that now Harriet is so effectively separated from Mr Robert Martin, the occupant of Abbey-Mill Farm, she is immune to its varying attractions over the course of the year – whether in spring, early summer, midsummer or autumn. What Austen offers us in this sentence is not Radcliffian haze, but a precise depiction, in the form of a miniature montage, of the turning seasons. Months may come and months may go, but Harriet will not again succumb to a mere farmer.

Is Oliver Dreaming?

The mysterious apparition of Fagin and Monks at the window outside the room where Oliver is dozing in the supposed safety of his country retreat with the Maylie family furnishes one of Cruikshank's memorable illustrations to *Oliver Twist*:

The circumstances surrounding this episode have been much worried over by commentators on the novel. The convalescent Oliver is described as being in his own little room, on the ground floor, at the back of the house. The situation is Edenic:

> It was quite a cottage-room, with a lattice-window: around which were clusters of jessamine and honeysuckle, that crept over the casement, and filled the place with their delicious perfume. It looked into a garden, whence a wicket-gate opened into a small paddock; all beyond was fine meadow-land and wood. There was no other dwelling near, in that direction; and the prospect it commanded was very extensive.
>
> One beautiful evening, when the first shades of twilight were beginning to settle upon the earth, Oliver sat at this window, intent upon his books. He had been poring over them for some time; and, as the day had been uncommonly sultry, and he had exerted himself a great deal, it is no disparagement to the authors, whoever they may have been, to say, that gradually and by slow degrees, he fell asleep.
>
> There is a kind of sleep that steals upon us sometimes, which, while it holds the body prisoner, does not free the mind from a sense of things about it, and enable it to ramble at its pleasure. So far as an overpowering heaviness, a prostration of strength, and an utter inability to control our thoughts or power of motion, can be called sleep, this is it; and yet we have a consciousness of all that is going on about us; and if we dream at such a time, words which are really spoken, or sounds which really exist at the moment, accommodate themselves with surprising readiness to our visions, until reality and imagination become so strangely blended that it is afterwards almost a matter of impossibility to separate the two. Nor is this, the most striking phenomenon incidental to such a state. It is an undoubted fact, that although our senses of touch and sight be for the time dead, yet our sleeping thoughts, and the visionary scenes that pass before us, will be influenced, and ma-

terially influenced, by the *mere silent presence* of some external object: which may not have been near us when we closed our eyes: and of whose vicinity we have had no waking consciousness.

Oliver knew, perfectly well, that he was in his own little room; that his books were lying on the table before him; and that the sweet air was stirring among the creeping plants outside. And yet he was asleep. Suddenly, the scene changed; the air became close and confined; and he thought, with a glow of terror, that he was in the Jew's house again. There sat the hideous old man, in his accustomed corner: pointing at him: and whispering to another man, with his face averted, who sat beside him.

'Hush, my dear!' he thought he heard the Jew say; 'it is he, sure enough. Come away.'

'He!' the other man seemed to answer; 'could I mistake him, think you? If a crowd of devils were to put themselves into his exact shape, and he stood amongst them, there is something that would tell me how to point him out. If you buried him fifty feet deep, and took me across his grave, I should know, if there wasn't a mark above it, that he lay buried there. I should!'

The man seemed to say this, with such dreadful hatred, that Oliver awoke with the fear, and started up.

Good Heaven! what was that, which sent the blood tingling to his heart, and deprived him of his voice, and of power to move! There – there – at the window; close before him; so close, that he could have almost touched him before he started back: with his eyes peering into the room, and meeting his: there stood the Jew! And beside him, white with rage, or fear, or both, were the scowling features of the very man who had accosted him at the inn-yard.

It was but an instant, a glance, a flash, before his eyes; and they were gone. But they had recognised him, and he them; and their look was as firmly impressed upon his memory, as if it had been deeply carved in stone, and set before him from his birth. He stood transfixed for a moment; and then, leaping from the window into the garden, called loudly for help.

Chapter 34 breaks off at this point. The next chapter opens with a general alarm at Oliver's cry ('The Jew! The Jew!'). Oliver points out the 'course the men had taken'. But, despite everyone's vigorous efforts, 'the search was all in vain. There were not even the traces of recent footsteps, to be seen.' The physical improbability of the two men having been in the area is pondered:

> They stood, now, on the summit of a little hill, commanding the open fields in every direction for three or four miles. There was the village in the hollow on the left; but, in order to gain that, after pursuing the track Oliver had pointed out, the men must have made a circuit of open ground, which it was impossible they could have accomplished in so short a time. A thick wood skirted the meadow-land in another direction; but they could not have gained that covert for the same reason.

But when Harry Maylie tells Oliver 'it must have been a dream,' the boy protests: 'Oh no . . . I saw him too plainly for that. I saw them both, as plainly as I see you now.' Enquiries are pursued, servants are despatched to ask questions at all the alehouses in the area, but nothing is turned up. Monks and Fagin have not been seen by another human eye in the neighbourhood, going or coming, although the appearance of two such low-life aliens would surely have attracted the notice of suspicious locals (as Monks immediately attracted Oliver's attention when he earlier ran into him at the nearby market town). Nor is the fact that the two men were actually at Oliver's window confirmed later in the story. Has Oliver imagined the whole thing? Was it a dream? By commissioning an illustration of the scene by Cruikshank, Dickens seems to support Oliver's insisted declaration – that it visibly and actually happened. The men *were* there at the window. Moreover, the conversation (particularly Monks's characteristically melodramatic expressions of hatred) rings very true in the reader's ear.

But, if one accepts the actuality of what Oliver saw, three problems follow: (1) How did Fagin and Monks discover where Oliver was staying? (2) How did the two men, neither of whom is notably agile, disappear so suddenly – before Oliver, who *is* agile and has jumped out of the window, can see where they have made off to? (3) Why did the interlopers leave no physical trace of their presence?

A number of explanations have been put forward. That Dickens was less careful in writing the novel than we are in reading it is the most primitive. Humphry House, in his introduction to the 1949 Oxford Illustrated edition of *Oliver Twist*, notes that Dickens wrote and published the work in a huge hurry, and that it 'was Dickens's first attempt at a novel proper. The sequence of the external events which befall Oliver [is] complicated and careless.' John Bayley elsewhere notes that Dickens repeats, in this window scene, material which is to be found earlier in the novel, at the beginning of Chapter 9 ('There is a drowsy state, between sleeping and waking . . .'). This recycling of material would support the view that Dickens was under severe pressure.[1] Another primitive explanation is that in the window episode Dickens is resorting to the crude tricks of the Gothic ghost story. There is, for instance, a parallel instance earlier when, as he conspires at midnight with Fagin, Monks sees 'the shadow of a woman, in a cloak and bonnet, pass along the wainscot like a breath!'. The two men search the whole house and find nothing – the woman, we apprehend, is the wraith of Oliver's mother, his protective angel.

Many critics prefer more ingenious readings. Steven Marcus, for example, in *Dickens: From Pickwick to Dombey* (London, 1965) examines the scene and its 'hypnagogic' references for Freudian clues that can be tracked back to Dickens's primal experiences in the blacking factory. J. Hillis Miller reads the scene for its demonstration of 'the total insecurity of Oliver's precarious happy state'. The vision of evil at the window is proof that his 'past is permanently part of him'. The absence of prints suggests that Fagin is to be equated with the similarly light-footed devil.[2]

Colin Williamson, reviewing these and other hypotheses, offers what he calls a more 'mundane' explanation.[3] He advocates reading *Oliver Twist* as one would a detective story or crime thriller. Williamson notes as significant a perplexing earlier episode in Chapter 32 in which Oliver is travelling to London with Mr Losberne to find the house of Mr Brownlow (Oliver can recall the street and the general aspect of the building, but not the number). Suddenly, at Chertsey Bridge, the excited boy turns very pale when he 'recognises' another house – that in which he and Sikes's gang hid before the attempted burglary. They stop the carriage and the impulsive Losberne bursts his way in. They encounter 'a little, ugly hump-backed man', who is understandably furious at the invasion of his property by these two strangers and vociferates horrific but comically impotent threats. There is, as it turns out, absolutely nothing to prove that the burglars were ever in the house. The furniture and interior decoration are entirely different from what Oliver remembers and has told his friends about: 'not even the position of the cupboards; answered Oliver's description!' Oliver and the doctor leave with the little man's curses ringing in their ears. Losberne is embarrassed by the whole episode, and evidently sees it as evidence of Oliver's extraordinary nervousness. None the less, the good-hearted doctor trusts the boy sufficiently to go looking for Brownlow's house, which they discover after a little trial and error. Oliver remembers the way to the street and recognises the house immediately by its white colour.

As Williamson points out, the odd thing about the business with the little ugly humpbacked man's house 'is its apparent pointlessness'. But, Williamson suggests,

if we approach *Oliver Twist* as a crime thriller, the obvious explanation of the confusion over the house is that the hunchback is an
associate of Sikes who allows him the use of the house for his
nefarious purposes, and that Dickens had planned that Losberne's
action in entering the house should give its occupant a chance to
see and identify Oliver . . . All the members of the gang would
doubtless have been alerted to Oliver's disappearance in the district and the threat he constituted to their safety; and it would be
easy enough for an astute hunchback to track Oliver down
through his companion and the carriage he occupied.

It is an attractive hypothesis – except that a bona fide thriller-
writer would surely have alerted the reader to the significance
of the event later in the story. Williamson implies that pressure of serialisation may have prevented Dickens from working
out this detail of the plot satisfactorily.

There are other logical objections. It would hardly be necessary for the gang to use accidental sources of information
and all the complicated business of trailing carriages many
miles into the countryside – assuming that the little man could
set the operation up before Losberne's carriage was on its way
into the maelstrom of the London streets. Since the wounded
Oliver was taken into the same house that was set up for the
burglary (an establishment that had been thoroughly 'cased' in
advance), and had remained there several weeks convalescing
from his bullet-wound, he could have been effortlessly tracked
by Sikes, who could have found his way to the scene of the
crime blindfolded. It is true that the Maylies have moved for
the summer to the country; but they have left servants in the
house who know the other address and have no reason for
keeping it secret. It would be the work of minutes for the Art-
ful Dodger to invent some ruse for being told where the
Maylie household and their little invalid guest are now resid-
ing. If there is a larger significance in the episode of the little
humpbacked man it is, surely, that despite this evidence of

Oliver's unreliability (and his whole story strains credulity to breaking-point) the good doctor and his friends persist in believing him. Although he clearly is in error about the gang's house, they trust that he can locate Brownlow's house. And, by implication, they believe his whole incredible story.

Yet another explanation of the window episode is offered by Fred Kaplan in *Dickens and Mesmerism* (Princeton, 1975). Kaplan notes that *Oliver Twist* was written at the height of 'The Mesmeric Mania', when Dickens was closely associated with the arch-apostle of this new science, Dr John Elliotson. The long disquisition about Oliver's half-sleeping sensory awareness seems a clear pointer to the author's current fascination with mesmerism and 'animal magnetism'. As Kaplan records, it was one of Elliotson's claims that 'the mesmerized subject can see with his eyes closed'. This would seem to be how Oliver becomes aware of the criminals at the window before he has woken from his sleep – which may more truly be described as a trance, or what the mesmerists called 'sleep-waking'. One could go one step farther (as Kaplan does not) and suggest that the whole episode is a mesmeric phenomenon. This would explain the lack of any footprints or visible signs of Fagin's and Monks's preternaturally sudden disappearance ('It was but an instant, a glance, a flash, before his eyes; and they were gone').

There is, as it happens, strong supporting evidence for the hypothesis that the whole episode is an example of what the practitioners of mesmerism called 'mental travelling'. It is not the case that Monks and Fagin visit Oliver; he visits *them*, borne on the wings of mesmeric trance. As Alison Winter has recorded, from August 1837 to May 1838 Elliotson carried out private experiments on many of his patients, and in particular the domestic servant, Elizabeth O'Key, in the wards of University College Hospital. In the spring and summer of 1838 he put on a series of public demonstrations at UCH. According to Kaplan, Dickens attended the first O'Key demonstration on

10 May 1838, or the second on 2 June, or 'perhaps even both'. As Winter describes the experiments: 'Elliotson did things such as mesmerizing her through walls from various distances; she had visions in which she represented herself as if she felt that various personages were around her – these individuals told her things which became personal prophecies.'4 There is also a notable similarity between the language of Dickens's remarks about Oliver's tranced sensitivity to absent personages, and what commentators were saying about O'Key in 1838.

Probably no explanation of this episode will convince everyone and some will convince no one. I would like, however, to offer an explanation of my own. *Oliver Twist* was first published as a serial in *Bentley's Miscellany*, from February 1837 to April 1839. It was an amazingly busy period in Dickens's early career. He had outstanding contracts for new novels and editorial commitments to no less than three different publishers, and felt that he was in danger of 'busting the boiler'.

One of the problems for the serialist working at full stretch was providing early enough copy for his illustrator, particularly if his partner (like George Cruikshank) needed to have his designs engraved on steel – a long and difficult procedure. When he had time in hand, Dickens preferred to supply manuscript or proofs to Cruikshank, so that he could portray narrative details accurately. But, as Kathleen Tillotson notes, 'although Dickens originally promised to let Cruikshank have the manuscript by the fifth of the month, the evidence suggests that after the first month he was always late, sometimes sending an instalment of manuscript, and sometimes conveying instructions for the illustration by a note or by word of mouth'.5

'Monks and the Jew' appeared in the *Bentley's* instalment for June 1838. Dickens felt himself particularly pressed at this point, because he thought copy was needed early, on account of the Coronation on the twenty-eighth of the month. My speculation is that before actually writing this section of the narrative Dickens foresaw an abduction or murder attempt on Oliver; and duly instructed Cruikshank to go ahead with the villains-at-the-window illustration, preparatory to that scenario. But, while writing the episode, Dickens settled on something more complex, bringing the Bumbles, Noah Claypole, and Bill Sikes back into the centre of things. It remains uncertain, *if* they are real, and not figments of Oliver's superheated imagination, what Fagin and Monks intend to do with the intelligence that Oliver is now lodged with the Maylies. But once Cruikshank had supplied the illustration, it was impossible, at this short notice, to procure another and Dickens suddenly realised that he could elegantly write himself out of the dilemma by means of the 'mesmeric enigma' device, using material gathered at the O'Key demonstrations.[6]

It would seem that Dickens's more scientific contemporaries registered the interesting overtones of the window scene in Chapter 34. G. H. Lewes wrote a letter (which has not survived) evidently enquiring exactly what Dickens had intended, and on what scientific authority the scene was devised. Towards the end of November 1838 Elliotson himself responded. Dickens wrote the following note to his illustrator:

> My Dear Cruikshank,
>   Elliotson has written to me to go and see some experiments on Okey [*sic*] at his house at 3 o'clock tomorrow afternoon. He begs me to invite you. Will you come? Let me know.
>   Ever Faithfully Yrs.[7]

Why, one may go on to wonder, did Dickens in later prefaces to the novel not alert the reader to the scientific plausibility of Oliver's clairvoyance as, for instance, he ferociously defended the 'spontaneous combustion' in *Bleak House*, when G. H. Lewes questioned it? There is a likely explanation. In September 1838 O'Key was denounced as an impostor by Thomas

Wakley in the *Lancet*. In the squabble that followed, Elliotson was forced to resign his position at UCH in late December of the same year. In the judgement of most intelligent lay persons (even those like Dickens who were friendly with Elliotson) the O'Key experiments, if not wholly discredited, had been rendered extremely dubious. In these circumstances, although he saw no reason to change his text, neither did Dickens see any good reason for drawing the reader's attention to the 'science' on which the window scene is based.

Is Heathcliff a Murderer?

When he returns to Wuthering Heights after his mysterious three-year period of exile Heathcliff has become someone very cruel. He left an uncouth but essentially humane stable-lad. He returns a gentleman psychopath. His subsequent brutalities are graphically recorded. They are many and very unpleasant. He humiliates Edgar Linton, who has married Cathy during his absence. 'I wish you joy of the milk-blooded coward,' he tells Cathy in her husband's presence. The taunt is the more brutal since Edgar is clearly the weaker man and in no position to exact physical reparation. Heathcliff goes on to torment Edgar by hinting that he has cuckolded him. Subsequently Heathcliff beats his wife Isabella, as he has gruesomely promised to do in an earlier conversation with Cathy: 'You'd hear of odd things, if I lived alone with that mawkish, waxen face; the most ordinary would be painting on its white the colours of the rainbow, and turning the blue eyes black, every day or two; they detestably resemble Linton's.'

When Nelly sees Isabella, after she has fled from Heathcliff, she does indeed describe 'a white face scratched and bruised'. Isabella goes on to describe her husband's 'murderous violence' to Nelly in some detail. Heathcliff has shaken her till her teeth rattle. He has thrown a kitchen knife at her head which 'struck beneath my ear'; she has a wound which will probably scar her for life. Had she not run away, who knows how far he would have gone in his cold brutality towards her.

In later life Heathcliff would certainly have beaten his son as savagely as he beat the boy's mother, were it not that he

needs the degenerate brat whole and unmarked for his long-term scheme of revenge against Thrushcross Grange. He has no compunction about punching young Catherine. Young Heathcliff tells Nelly about his father's violent reaction on learning that the girl has tried to keep for herself two miniatures of her dead parents:

'I said *they* were mine, too; and tried to get them from her. The spiteful thing wouldn't let me; she pushed me off, and hurt me. I shrieked out – that frightens her – she heard papa coming, and she broke the hinges, and divided the case and gave me her mother's portrait; the other she attempted to hide; but papa asked what was the matter and I explained it. He took the one I had away, and ordered her to resign hers to me; she refused, and he – he struck her down, and wrenched it off the chain, and crushed it with his foot.'

'And were you pleased to see her struck?' I asked: having my designs in encouraging his talk.

'I winked,' he answered. 'I wink to see my father strike a dog, or a horse, he does it so hard.'

Or a woman, one may add. It is not just four-footed victims who feel the weight of Heathcliff's fist.

Heathcliff is capable of more cold-blooded and calculating cruelty. He abducts young Catherine and keeps her from her dying father's bedside, accelerating Edgar's death and ensuring that it shall be an extremely miserable one. He urges Hindley towards self-destruction by encouraging his fatal mania for drink and cards. On a casual level, Heathcliff is given to killing household pets (he strangles his wife's favourite dog by way of a wedding present) and desecrates graves.

Mr Heathcliff, we may assume, is not a nice man. And in a later age his violence and lawlessness would have earned him a prison sentence – or at the very least a string of restraining orders and court injunctions. But does Heathcliff commit the cruellest crime of all, murder?

To answer this question we must examine the suspicious circumstances of the death of Hindley Earnshaw, master of Wuthering Heights. 'The end of Earnshaw was what might have been expected,' Nelly recalls in her long narrative to Lockwood, 'it followed fast on his sister's, there was scarcely six months between them. We, at the Grange, never got a very succinct account of his state preceding it.' Nelly learns of the death, after the event, from the local apothecary, Mr Kenneth. 'He died true to his character,' Kenneth cheerfully adds, 'drunk as a lord.' Hindley was just twenty-seven. Evidently Kenneth has witnessed the death and signed the necessary certificate.

Nelly's suspicions are immediately aroused. 'Had he fair play?' she ponders. The anxiety 'bothers' her and she makes a trip to Wuthering Heights to discover what she can of the truth of the case. Before going she learns from Earnshaw's lawyer (who also acts for Mr Linton, Nelly's employer) that the 'whole property [of Wuthering Heights] is mortgaged' – to Heathcliff.[1] At the Heights, Nelly meets Heathcliff who, rather shiftily, as we may think, gives his eyewitness account of Hindley's death:

'That fool's body should be buried at the cross-roads, without ceremony of any kind [i.e. Hindley committed suicide] – I happened to leave him ten minutes, yesterday afternoon; and, in that interval, he fastened the two doors of the house against me, and he has spent the night in drinking himself to death deliberately! We broke in this morning, for we heard him snorting like a horse; and there he was, laid over a settle – flaying and scalping would not have wakened him – I sent for Kenneth, and he came; but not till the beast had changed into carrion – he was both dead and cold, and stark; and so you'll allow, it was useless making more stir about him!'

By the last enigmatic remark, Heathcliff means that it would have been 'useless' calling in the coroner, on the grounds that the death was suspicious.

Heathcliff's account is 'confirmed' to Nelly by Joseph, the misanthropic (but wholly reliable) old manservant at the Heights. Joseph, however, is by no means happy about his former master's last hours:

'Aw'd rayther he'd goan hisseln fur t'doctor! Aw sud uh taen tent uh t'maister better nur him – un' he warn't deead when Aw left, nowt uh t'soart!' ['I would rather that Heathcliff had gone himself for the doctor! I should have taken care of the master better than him – and he wasn't dead when I left, nothing of the sort!'].

Joseph is invincibly honest. And one concurs in his 'muttered' doubts (he dare not voice them out loud, in case Heathcliff hears, and gives him the back of his hand). It is most improbable that a twenty-seven-year-old man, in otherwise robust health, should be able to 'drink himself to death' in a single night. Young men do, of course, kill themselves by excessive drinking, but usually by driving cars drunk, or by inhaling their own vomit while sleeping. It is clear that – although he is 'snorting' – Hindley is breathing efficiently when he is left alone with Heathcliff. Did he show signs of being about to suffocate, it would be an easy thing for Heathcliff to lift him up and bang him on the back, thus clearing his throat. And, as Joseph recalls, although dead drunk, Hindley did not appear to be dying. He was, however, insensible and incapable of resisting anyone stifling him with a cushion. Kenneth is a somewhat elusive figure, but it is likely that as a mere apothecary ('Mr' Kenneth) he would not have been able to conduct any expert medical examination of the body. It may even be that Heathcliff bribed him to sign the certificate and obviate any embarrassing coroner's inquest.

It is nicely poised and every reader must make his or her own judgement. If Heathcliff did stifle Hindley (albeit that Hindley has earlier tried to shoot and stab Heathcliff) we have to see him as a sociopathic monster. If he watched the man die, and declined to prevent his death (by clearing Hindley's throat, for example) he is scarcely better. These plausible reconstructions of what happened at Wuthering Heights while Heathcliff and the incapable Hindley were alone together render absurd such rosy adaptations as the Samuel Goldwyn 1939 film (the Goldwyn screenplay, by Ben Hecht and Charles MacArthur, ends with Heathcliff, played by Laurence Olivier, and Cathy, played by Merle Oberon, reunited as carefree ghosts skipping merrily over Penistone Crags). If we believe that Heathcliff was simply an innocent bystander at Hindley's self-destruction, then we can credit the sympathetic reading of his character suggested by the exclamation Nelly overhears him make, in the intensity of his wretchedness: 'I have no pity! I have no pity! The [more the] worms writhe, the more I yearn to crush out their entrails! It is a moral teething, and I grind with greater energy, in proportion to the increase of pain.'

When a baby savagely bites its teething ring, it is because it (the baby) is experiencing excruciating pain from the teeth tearing their way through its gums. So Heathcliff may be seen to inflict pain on others (hurling knives at his wife, taunting Edgar, striking young Catherine, lashing his horse) only because he feels greater inward pain himself. But one cannot so justify the furtive smothering, in cold blood, of someone whose death will mean considerable financial gain to the murderer.

There are no clear answers to this puzzle. As Ian Jack has noted, '*Wuthering Heights* is one of the most enigmatic of English novels.' Whether or not Heathcliff is guilty of capital crime remains a fascinating but ultimately inscrutable enigma at the very heart of the narrative. For what it is worth, I believe he *did* kill Hindley, although for any unprejudiced jury it is likely that enough 'reasonable doubt' would remain to acquit him.

Villette's *Double Ending*

Critics have traditionally been fascinated by the enigmatic ending of *Villette* – particularly hyper-modern critics who see in the novel an anticipation of the 'problematised text', so beloved of deconstructionists and of theorists generally. To summarise: at the end of the narrative, Lucy Snowe has her virtuous pluck rewarded by the declared love and marriage proposals of her stern 'professor', Paul Emanuel. But before he can make Lucy his wife, Paul must spend three years working in the French protectorate Guadeloupe. The reasons for his exile to this far-off place are vaguely communicated to the reader by Lucy, in Chapter 39: 'its alpha is Mammon, and its omega Interest,' she declares. Madame Walravens, we are informed, has earlier inherited by marriage a large estate at Basseterre, on the West Indian island: 'if duly looked after by a competent agent of integrity' for 'a few years', the estate will be 'largely productive'. Madame Walravens asks Paul to be her 'competent agent'. As Lucy observes, such a wish is a command: 'No living being ever humbly laid his advantage at M. Emanuel's feet, or confidingly put it into his hands, that he spurned the trust, or repulsed the repository.' Whatever might be Paul's 'private pain or inward reluctance to leave Europe', he accedes.

It is, on the face of it, strange that Paul should accede. The claims of Lucy and his own happiness would seem to be stronger than the financial convenience of Madame Walravens. He is not, in any case, a businessman, but a schoolteacher and a very good one – if a little too fond of 'discipline'. But it is not hard to deduce what duties Paul Emanuel is required for. The date of *Villette*'s action is the early 1840s (the period of Charlotte Brontë's own residence in Brussels, 1842–4). Slavery had finally been abolished in the British West Indies in 1833, precipitating a disastrous collapse in the sugar industry, with the widespread defection of pressed labour. In neighbouring Guadeloupe, under the unenlightened French imperial regime, the institution of slavery (and the profitability of the sugar plantations) was to limp along until its eventual, long-overdue abolition in 1848. The stern and dictatorial Professor Emanuel – the bully of Madame Beck's classroom – has been recruited to rally the increasingly dissident slave labourers of Madame Walravens's estate, with whips and scorpions, if necessary. For 'competent', read 'brutal'. There is another putative factor in the virtuous lady's choosing Monsieur Emanuel as her overseer. He has shown himself, in his attendance at Madame Beck's establishment, remarkably capable of restraining himself sexually in the presence of nubile young women. All nineteenth-century accounts of Guadeloupe stress that it is a place of almost irresistible temptation for European males. As the *Encyclopaedia Britannica* (14th edition, 1929) records:

> Guadeloupe has a few white officials and planters, a few East Indian immigrants from the French possessions in India, and the rest negroes and mulattoes. These mulattoes are famous for their grace and beauty of both form and feature. Women greatly outnumber men, and illegitimate births are very numerous.

Clearly only a man of iron self-discipline can be trusted in such a Sodom.

One assumes that Paul's motives for exiling himself from Lucy are at least partly to test his bride-to-be, to try her ability to survive without him. Is she worthy to be Madame Emanuel? He is fond of imposing such ordeals. In the three years of his absence Lucy must prove her worth by setting up a school. She succeeds magnificently, inspired by the lessons in discipline and self-discipline that she has learned from her professor.

The relationship between the lovers during Paul's absence is sustained by passionate letters. The novel concludes with a coda which switches dramatically from the past to the present tense: 'And now the three years are past. M. Emanuel's return is fixed.' It was early summer when he left (the roses were in bloom). Now, on the eve of his return, it is autumn and the season of equinoctial storms. Lucy apostrophises the elements as her demonic foe:

> The wind shifts to the west. Peace, peace, Banshee – 'keening' at every window! It will rise – it will swell – it shrieks out long: wander as I may through the house this night, I cannot lull the blast. The advancing hours make it strong: by midnight, all sleepless watchers hear and fear a wild south-west storm.

A cataclysmic storm duly rages for seven days, an appropriately de-creating span of time which will, we fear, return Lucy's universe to chaos. The novel concludes with two enigmatic and emotionally exhausted last paragraphs:

> Here pause: pause at once. There is enough said. Trouble no quiet, kind heart; leave sunny imaginations hope. Let it be theirs to conceive the delight of joy born again fresh out of great terror, the rapture of rescue from peril, the wondrous reprieve from dread, the fruition of return. Let them picture union and a happy succeeding life.
>
> Madame Beck prospered all the days of her life; so did Père Silas; Madame Walravens fulfilled her ninetieth year before she died. Farewell.

Does Emanuel drown or does he survive drowning? The reference to Madame Walravens indicates that Lucy is writing many years after the event, so the outcome must be known – despite the present tense used to evoke the storm.

The novel's internal structure of allusion is enigmatic on the question. The 'Banshee' reference looks all the way back to Chapter 4, which features a terrible storm while Lucy is in England, in the service of the invalid Miss Marchmont. That storm is described as being accompanied by a 'subtle screeching cry'. Looking forward, beyond the events of *Villette*'s narrative, Lucy records that:

> Three times in the course of my life, events had taught me that these strange accents in the storm – this restless, hopeless cry – denote a coming state of the atmosphere unpropitious to life. Epidemic diseases, I believed, were often heralded by a gasping, sobbing, tormented long-lamenting east wind. Hence, I inferred, arose the legend of the Banshee.

Miss Marchmont dies that night.

The second of the three occasions alluded to by Lucy in the above passage is recorded in Chapter 15. The heroine is now in the less congenial service of Madame Beck. She has been subject to 'peculiarly agonizing depression' and feverish delirium. Recovered from her nightmares, but still weak, she arises from her bed, unable to bear the 'solitude and the stillness' of the dormitory any longer. It is evening, and the darkening sky is terrible with the threat of storm:

> from the lattice I saw coming night-clouds trailing low like banners drooping. It seemed to me that at this hour there was affection and sorrow in Heaven above for all pain suffered on earth beneath; the weight of my dreadful dream became alleviated.

Lucy unwisely ventures out into the storm in her weakened, semi-invalid state. The end of this chapter marks the gap between the first and second volumes of the original three-volume edition brought out by Smith, Elder & Co in January 1853. For the mass of circulating-library readers, rationed by their one-guinea subscriptions to one volume at a time, this gap would entail more than simply reaching for the next volume. There would, probably, be a longish interval during which Volume I was returned (possibly after a delay while some other member of the family read it) and the second volume borrowed from the library (possibly after yet another delay if one had to visit Mudie's main establishment in Bloomsbury, or if all the second volumes were 'out'). Readers, thus kept in suspense, might reasonably expect that Lucy was about to die. Chapter 15 and Volume I end with the dramatic statement: 'I seemed to pitch headlong down an abyss. I remember no more.'

Is Lucy dead? Almost dead, it transpires. The opening of the second volume (Chapter 16) picks up on the 'abyss' reference: 'Where my soul went during that swoon I cannot tell.' Lucy has experienced, it seems, an after-death experience:

Whatever [my soul] saw, or wherever she travelled in her trance on that strange night, she kept her own secret; never whispering a word to Memory, and baffling Imagination by an indissoluble silence. She may have gone upward, and come in sight of her eternal home, hoping for leave to rest now, and deeming that her painful union with matter was at last dissolved. While she so deemed, an angel may have warned her away from heaven's threshold, and, guiding her weeping down, have bound her, once more, all shuddering and unwilling, to that poor frame, cold and wasted, of whose companionship she was grown more than weary.

Miss Soul's return (that is to say, Lucy's revival) is further metaphorised in terms of a painful rescue from drowning. This, one assumes, is the second 'Banshee' experience in which the victim is pulled back from the very jaws of death. The third Banshee-storm-death episode is that connected with Paul Emanuel's return voyage from Guadeloupe and his shipwreck at sea. Does it betoken death (as with Miss Marchmont) or a terrifying brush with death (as with Lucy)?

Charlotte Brontë evidently received some querulous correspondence on the subject of her indeterminate ending. As Mrs Gaskell records in her *Life of Charlotte Brontë*, two of the author's female contemporaries wrote demanding 'exact and authentic information respecting the fate of M. Paul Emanuel'. Brontë wrote to her editor at Smith, Elder & Co. saying she had despatched an answer, 'so worded as to leave the matter pretty much where it was. Since the little puzzle amuses the ladies, it would be a pity to spoil their sport by giving them the key.'

As Margaret Smith and Herbert Rosengarten suggest, in their Oxford World's Classics edition of *Villette*, we should also consider in this context Brontë's sharper letter to her publisher, George Smith, on 26 March 1853:

With regard to that momentous point – M. Paul's fate – in case anyone in future should request to be enlightened thereon – they may be told that it was designed that every reader should settle the catastrophe for himself, according to the quality of his disposition, the tender or remorseful impulse of his nature. Drowning and Matrimony are the fearful alternatives. The Merciful . . . will of course choose the former and milder doom – drown him to put him out of pain. The cruel-hearted will on the contrary pitilessly impale him on the second horn of the dilemma – marrying him without ruth or compunction to that – person – that – that – individual – 'Lucy Snowe'.

Charlotte Brontë supplies us in this sarcastic letter with the 'key to the puzzle'. That is to say, one could only sustain the 'sunny' reading of the novel's ending if one equated the disaster of Paul's drowning with the 'disaster' of his marrying the woman he loves and who loves him. It is 'moral' for Lucy to prevaricate if Paul Emanuel has indeed died at sea, so as not to discomfit her less emotionally sturdy readers. Hiding her misery is a brave and admirable thing to do. Had Paul Emanuel returned, it would have been reprehensible to have disguised or withheld the fact. Such behaviour could only be construed as a claim for undeserved pity and sympathy.

There is, in short, no problem with the conclusion of *Villette*, if one gives it a moment's thought. Paul Emanuel drowns – end of story (literally). Mrs Gaskell confirms the point by reference to privileged family testimony:

Mr Brontë was anxious that her new tale should end well, as he disliked novels which left a melancholy impression upon the mind; and he requested her to make her hero and heroine (like the heroes and heroines in fairy-tales) 'marry, and live happily ever after'. But the idea of M. Paul Emanuel's death at sea was stamped on her imagination, till it assumed the distinct force of reality; and she could no more alter her fictitious ending than if they had been facts which she was relating. All she could do in compliance with her father's wish was so to veil the fate in oracular words, as to leave it to the character and discernment of her readers to interpret her meaning.

The interpretation is simple enough, and few sensible readers of the novel can have given credence to the spurious 'sunny' ending. More interesting – particularly in the context of 1853 – is the device of the double ending, the reader being left free to choose between a 'real' or a 'fairy-tale' version. *Villette* came out in January 1853. In October of the same year Thackeray began to serialise *The Newcomes*. This massive saga-novel was to continue as a monthly serial for the following twenty-three months, until August 1855. The main strand of Thackeray's narrative deals with the careers of the cousins Ethel and Clive Newcome, their true love for each other, and their respective unhappy marriages to less congenial partners.

The Newcomes ends with one of the greatest effusions of pathos in Victorian fiction, the death of Colonel Newcome, and Clive and Ethel aching for each other but for ever separated. There follows a coda in which Thackeray, apparently *in propria persona*, declares that: 'Two years ago, walking with my children in some pleasant fields, near to Berne, in Switzerland, I strayed from them into a little wood: and, coming out of it presently, told them how the story had been revealed to me somehow, which for three-and-twenty months the reader has been pleased to follow.'

Thackeray then embarks on an extended fantasia about what his characters are doing in 'Fable-land'. His belief is, he says, 'that in Fable-land somewhere Ethel and Clive are living most comfortably together'. That is, as man and wife. 'You', Thackeray tells his reader:

may settle your fable-land in your own fashion. Anything you like happens in fable-land. Wicked folks die à propos . . . annoying folks are got out of the way; the poor are rewarded – the upstarts are set down in fable-land . . . the poet of fable-land . . . makes the hero and heroine happy at last, and happy ever after. Ah, happy, harmless fable-land, where these things are! Friendly reader! may you and the author meet there on some future day! He hopes so; as he yet keeps a lingering hold of your hand, and bids you farewell with a kind heart.

It seems an uncannily close echo of the Revd Brontë's demand that his daughter's novel should deny its own character, and conclude with a 'fairy-tale' ending. And there is, as it happens, a graphic record of just such pressure being brought to bear on Thackeray. While lecturing in Coventry during the course of the serial run of *The Newcomes*, Thackeray was entertained by the Brays and Hennells (George Eliot's friends). Miss Hennell, as the ladies' spokeswoman, said:

'Mr Thackeray, we want you to let Clive marry Ethel. Do let them be happy.' He was surprised at their interest in his characters [and replied] 'The characters once created *lead me*, and I follow where they direct.'[1]

None the less, in his fable-land coda, as had Charlotte Brontë a couple of years earlier, Thackeray threw a sop to his soft-hearted readers and Coventry's imperious need for 'sunny' endings.

In April 1854, just over a year after *Villette*'s publication and a good year before the end of *The Newcomes*' run, Dickens began to serialise his new novel *Hard Times* in *Household Words*, where it ran weekly until August. *Hard Times* finishes with a visionary coda in which the narrator pictures a series of happy endings, including that of Louisa, released from Bounderby and again a wife – a mother – lovingly watchful of her children, ever careful that they should have a childhood of the mind no less than a childhood of the body, as knowing it to be even a more beautiful thing, and a possession, any hoarded scrap of which, is a blessing and happiness to the wisest.

'Did Louisa see this?' the narrator asks: 'Such a thing was never to be.'

These three novels, by the three leading novelists of 1853–5, all employ the same striking terminal device of the double ending. One of those double endings is harshly 'realistic', and aimed at tough readers (with whom the novelist is clearly in closer sympathy). For softer minded readers, of 'sunny' disposition, an alternative 'fairy-tale' ending is supplied (or in Dickens's case, hinted) in which Paul Emanuel returns to the embraces of his little Protestant Lucy, Clive and Ethel are united to the clashing peals of wedding bells, and Louisa recovers from her near seduction by Harthouse to become a respectably fulfilled materfamilias. 'You pays your money and you takes your pick,' the novels seem to say.

One can suggest a reason for this epidemic of double endings in 1853–5. Clearly Charlotte Brontë, Charles Dickens and Thackeray were responding to the pressure of a new reading public, one that wanted happy endings and could make its wants felt. That reading public (with its representative spokespersons like the Revd Brontë and Miss Hennell) had been massively organised and empowered by the new phenomenon of the circulating library – notably Mudie's. Charles Mudie's 'Leviathan' had started modestly enough in Southampton Row in the 1840s. In 1852, however, the firm moved into massive new premises at the corner of New Oxford Street and Museum Street. As Guinevere Griest records: 'During the ten years between 1853 and 1862, Mudie added almost 960,000 volumes to his library, nearly half of which were fiction.'[2] Mudie was suddenly the biggest bulk purchaser of new novels in the kingdom. And the

proprietor of the Leviathan demanded happy endings, on be-
half of his customers. As Griest again records, 'Over and over
again works were censured because they were "disagreeable"
or "unpleasant", qualities which Mr Mudie's readers did not
care to find in their novels.'

The peremptory demands of the library readers for sunshine
and their resentment of anything 'disagreeable' were beginning to be focused on the novelist in 1853–5, by direct pressure
from the publisher, himself under direct pressure from the
bulk-buying libraries. What the endings of these three high-
profile novels of the period indicate is that on their part the
novelists had registered the demands of this newly mobilised
force of library readers, and were devising subtle strategies of
resistance. This complex tug-of-war between novelist and
tyrannic circulating library was to continue until 1894 and the
collapse of the three-decker novel under the assault of novelists like George Moore and Thomas Hardy, enraged by the
constraints that Mrs Grundy (alias Mr Mudie, the 'nursemaid'
of literature) was imposing on their art and their claims to the
privileges of realism.

The Missing Fortnight

On its publication in three-volume form in August 1860 (after its triumphant nine-month serialisation in *All the Year Round*) *The Woman in White* enjoyed a huge success, sparking off what today we would call a sales mania and a franchise boom. As Wilkie Collins's biographer Kenneth Robinson records:

> While the novel was still selling in its thousands, manufacturers were producing *The Woman in White* perfume, *The Woman in White* cloaks and bonnets, and the music shops displayed *The Woman in White* waltzes and quadrilles . . . Dickens was not alone in his enthusiasm. Thackeray sat up all night reading it. Edward FitzGerald read it three times, and named a herring-lugger he owned *Marian Halcombe*, 'after the brave girl in the story'. The Prince Consort admired it greatly and sent a copy to Baron Stockmar.[1]

Nuel Davis, in his life of Collins, goes so far as to claim that '*The Woman in White* was probably the most popular novel written in England during the nineteenth century.'[2] This is demonstrably untrue (*Robert Elsmere* and *Trilby* outsold Collins's novel by many times), but it is quite likely that it was the best-seller of the decade.

Among the chorus of applause there was one discordant voice. *The Woman in White* received a devastating review in *The Times* (then, as now, the country's newspaper of record) on 30 October 1860. In the review E. S. Dallas proved – by close scrutiny of dates in the crucial Blackwater Park episodes – that the events described in the novel *could never have happened*. *The Woman in White* was, Dallas demonstrated, 'impossible'. As Dallas pointed out, the whole of Collins's intricate denouement hinges on a single date – when was it that Laura took her fateful trip to London in late July 1850? If it can be proved that the date of Laura's journey from Blackwater to Waterloo Station post-dated her recorded 'death' (in fact, the death of her lookalike half-sister, Anne Catherick) at 5 Forest Road, St John's Wood, then the criminals' conspiracy falls to the ground. With this crucial fact in mind, Dallas dismantled the plot machinery of *The Woman in White* with the ruthless precision of a prosecuting counsel exploding a shaky alibi:

The question of a date is the pivot upon which the novel turns. The whole of the third volume is devoted to the ascertaining of this date. Everything depends upon it. But it is lost in the most marvellous obscurity – it is lost even to Mr Wilkie Collins, who is a whole fortnight out of his reckoning. If we dare trespass upon details after the author's solemn injunction [in his preface to the three-volume edition, that reviewers not give away the plot] we could easily show that Lady Glyde could not have left Blackwater Park before the 9th or 10th of August. Anybody who reads the story and who counts the days from the conclusion of Miss Halcombe's diary, can verify the calculation for himself. He will find that the London physician did not pay his visit till the 31st of July, that Dawson [the doctor who attends on Marian] was not dismissed till the 3rd of August, and that the servants were not dismissed till the following day. The significance of these dates will be clear to all who have read the story. They render the last volume a mockery, a delusion, and a snare; and all the incidents in it are not merely improbable – they are absolutely impossible.[3]

The details of Dallas's criticism are less important than its general thrust. What he was doing, and doing brilliantly, was subjecting a work of fiction to the criterion of falsifiability, in terms of its internal logic and structure. This test was something distinctly new in literary criticism, and a corollary of the

fetishistic standards of documentary accuracy which Collins
had imported into English fiction as his hallmark. As he says in
his 'Preamble', Collins wanted his novel to be read as so many
pieces of evidence, 'as the story of an offence against the laws
is told in Court by more than one witness'. The reader, that is,
should be as alert to clues and discrepancies in evidence as is a
jury sitting in judgment. As Henry James astutely observed,
Collins was playing a deep game with genre and literary dis-
course. Collins's novels, James declared, were 'not so much
works of art as works of science. To read *The Woman in White*
requires very much the same intellectual effort as to read Mot-
ley or Froude.'4

What James implied by comparing Collins to the leading
historians of the age was that one could bring the same truth-
tests to *The Woman in White* that a sceptical expert might
bring to *The Rise of the Dutch Republic* (1855) or the *History
of England from the Death of Cardinal Wolsey to the Defeat of
the Spanish Armada* (12 vols, 1856–70). By reading *The Woman
in White* as if it were history or science (rather than just a
made-up story) Dallas can 'disprove' it.

Collins took Dallas's criticisms immensely seriously. He wrote
to his publisher the next day, instructing that no more copies
of *The Woman in White* must be put out, until he should have
an opportunity to revise the text: 'The critic in "The Times"
is (between ourselves) right about the mistake in time . . .
we will set it right at the first opportunity,' he confessed.5 The
mistake was duly set right in the 'New' 1861 one-volume
edition by antedating the crucial Blackwater Park episode a
whole sixteen days, and by clipping a couple of days off the crucial death-of-Anne/arrival-of-Laura episode (i.e. making it 25/26
July, rather than 28/29 July). In the revised edition, Collins
made other small corrections (changing the wedding date of
Percival Glyde and Laura, for instance, so that it did not hit a
Sunday in the 1849 calendar – a document which the novelist
evidently went back to consult in the course of revision).

Although he took extraordinary pains to reconcile fine points of narrative chronology, Collins left one mote to trouble the reader's eye. In the revised 1861 text, a day or two after 20 June, when Marian falls into her fever, Count Fosco discovers Anne Catherick's whereabouts and treats her heart condition. Having won her confidence, the fat villain passes on to Anne a forged message from Laura, telling her to go to London with her old friend and companion, Mrs Clements. Laura, Anne is reassured, will meet her there. Three days later, Anne having been strengthened sufficiently by Fosco's medicines to undertake the journey, the two women leave for London, where they take lodgings. 'A little more than a fortnight' after this (as Mrs Clements later testifies) Anne is abducted. By Mrs Clements's reckoning, this must be around 7 July – two to three weeks before Anne's death. But, by Fosco's account in his final written confession to Hartright, it was on 24 July that Anne Catherick was abducted and brought to the house in St John's Wood as 'Lady Laura Glyde'. The unfortunate woman died of heart failure there the next day, 25 July, and it was not until the day after that, 26 July, that the true Laura was lured to London. On 27 July she was returned to the London lunatic asylum as 'Anne Catherick', the true Anne Catherick now being prepared for her funeral at Limmeridge on 2 August, as 'Laura'.[6]

Who do we believe? Mrs Clements, by whose account Anne was in the sinister custody of the Foscos and the Rubelles for two weeks? Or Count Fosco, by whose account Anne was in their custody for two days? It does not require much inspection to see that Fosco's confession, for all its superficial candour, is shot through with self-serving falsehoods. Mrs Clements, by contrast, is stolidly honest. In terms of character the reader/jury will find her by far the more credible witness. And if Anne was held for two weeks in St John's Wood, what was she subjected to during that time? A clue is supplied in the famous anecdote of the novel's inspiration, given by J. G. Millais (the painter's son), ten years after Collins's death:

One night in the '50s [John Everett] Millais was returning
home to 83, Gower Street from one of the many parties held
under Mrs Collins's hospitable roof in Hanover Terrace, and,
in accordance with the usual practice of the two brothers, Wilkie
and Charles [Collins], they accompanied him on his homeward
walk through the dimly-lit, and those days semi-rural, roads
and lanes of North London . . . It was a beautiful moonlight
night in the summer time and as the three friends walked along
chatting gaily together, they were suddenly arrested by a piercing
scream coming from the garden of a villa close at hand. It was
evidently the cry of a woman in distress; and while pausing to
consider what they should do, the iron gate leading to the garden
was dashed open, and from it came the figure of a young and
very beautiful woman dressed in flowing white robes that shone
in the moonlight. She seemed to float rather than run in their
direction, and, on coming up to the three men, she paused for
a moment in an attitude of supplication and terror. Then, suddenly seeming to recollect herself, she suddenly moved on and
vanished in the shadows cast upon the road. 'What a lovely
woman!' was all Millais could say. 'I must see who she is, and what
is the matter,' said Wilkie Collins, as, without a word, he dashed
off after her. His two companions waited in vain for his return,
and next day, when they met again, he seemed indisposed to talk
of his adventure. They gathered from him, however, that he had
come up with the lovely fugitive and had heard from her own lips
the history of her life and the cause of her sudden flight. She was
a young lady of good birth and position, who had accidentally
fallen into the hands of a man living in a villa in Regent's Park.
There for many months he kept her prisoner under threats and
mesmeric influence of so alarming a character that she dared not
attempt to escape, until, in sheer desperation, she fled from the
brute, who, with a poker in his hand, threatened to dash her
brains out. Her subsequent history, interesting as it is, is not for
these pages.[7]

Fosco, we remember, is a mesmerist: the Rubelles are thugs. What we can plausibly suppose is that, like the other luckless Woman in White, Anne was incarcerated for quite some time in a villa in the Regent's Park district, where she was subjected to barbarous mistreatment, which may well have included sexual abuse. It was this mistreatment which provoked her death from heart failure on 25 July. Fosco, out of guilt, suppresses the fact that he was responsible for Anne's death by torture, claiming instead that she died of 'natural causes', having been in his care only a few hours.

There is, of course, a simpler explanation – namely that Collins simply made another chronological miscalculation. But this seems unlikely. He revised the time-scheme of *The Woman in White* so conscientiously for the 1861 text, and he was so expert in such dovetailing, that it is much more attractive to assume that he left the anomaly for his more detectively inclined readers to turn up. This reading elite should have the privilege of knowing just how subtle and evil the Napoleon of Crime, Count Fosco, really was.

Is Will Ladislaw Legitimate?

It helps to picture the dramatis personae of *Middlemarch* less as a community of English townspeople of the early nineteenth century than as a Papuan tribe – each connected to the other by complex ties of blood and marriage. Unknotting these ties requires the skills of the anthropologist rather than those of the literary critic. Let us start with Casaubon. Early in the narrative, the middle-aged vicar of Lowick is most vexed when Mr Brooke (making unwarranted deductions from their age difference) refers to young Will Ladislaw as 'your nephew'. Will, as Casaubon testily points out, is his 'second cousin', not his nephew. We learn from questions which Dorothea asks on her first visit to Lowick that Casaubon's mother, whose Christian and maiden names we never know, had an elder sister, Julia. This Aunt Julia – as we much later learn – ran away to marry a Polish patriot called Ladislaw and was disinherited by her family. Julia and her husband had one child, as best we can make out. Ladislaw Jr. (we never learn his first name) inherited from his father a musical gift which the son turned to use in the theatre – to little profit, apparently. In this capacity he met an actress, Sarah Dunkirk. Sarah, like Casaubon's Aunt Julia, had run away from her family's household to go on the stage. At some point before or after running away, she discovered that her father, Archie Dunkirk, who at one point in the text is alleged to be Jewish (although a practising Nonconformist Christian of the severest kind), was engaged in criminal activities. He is reported to have had a respectable pawnbroking business in Highbury, and another establishment which fenced stolen goods in the West End. Sarah broke off all relations with her mother and father on making this discovery. They had another child, a boy, and effectively disowned their disobedient daughter.

Sarah was subsequently married to, or set up house with, Ladislaw Jr. The couple had one child (Will) before the father prematurely succumbed to an unidentified wasting disease. Before dying, he introduced himself to Edward Casaubon, who generously undertook to take care of the penniless widow and child. Will is too young to remember anything distinctly about his father. On her part, Mrs Ladislaw died in 1825, some ten years after her husband, of what is vaguely described as a 'fall'.

At some point after Sarah Dunkirk's breaking off all relations with her parents, her brother died. Shortly after this her father also died. In the distress of her double bereavement, Mrs Dunkirk (now an old lady, and – although she does not know it – a grandmother) turned to a young evangelical clerk of her husband's, called Nicholas Bulstrode. Eventually, she married the young man. The disparity in age precluded children. As she approached death, a distraught Mrs Bulstrode made desperate attempts to locate her daughter Sarah with the hope of reconciliation. But, although he had discovered their whereabouts, Bulstrode – assisted in his act of deception by another former employee of Dunkirk's, John Raffles – suppressed all information about Sarah and her little boy. Raffles in fact makes contact with Sarah twice, although he only informs Bulstrode about the first encounter (this is important since, for complicated reasons, he only discovers Ladislaw's name on the second occasion). When Mrs Bulstrode died, Bulstrode, by his act of deception, inherited his wife's entire fortune and used it to set up a bank in Middlemarch. It will help at this point to refer to a family tree (see Fig. 1). As Farebrother puts it with uncharacteristic coarseness later in the narrative (presumably echoing Middlemarch gossip): 'our mercurial Ladislaw has a queer genealogy! A high spirited young lady and a musical Polish patriot made a likely enough stock for him to spring from, but I should never have suspected a grafting of the Jew pawnbroker.'

This means, of course, that Bulstrode is Casaubon's distant cousin by marriage – although both are oblivious of the relationship. In Middlemarch, the still-young, newly widowed, and now rich Nicholas Bulstrode married Harriet Vincy. She is a sister of Walter Vincy, manufacturer, husband to Lucy Vincy and father of the novel's *jeunes premiers* Fred and Rosamond. Mrs Vincy's sister was the second wife of the rich skinflint, Peter Featherstone. Featherstone's first wife was a sister of Caleb Garth, father of Mary Garth and other children who feature on the edge of the novel's plot. Peter Featherstone has no child by either of these two wives, both of whom predecease him by some years. But, unknown to his hopeful heirs (among whom the most hopeful is his nephew Fred Vincy), Peter Featherstone had a third, common-law wife, called Rigg. By this Miss Rigg, Featherstone has an illegitimate son, Joshua, born in 1798. Discarded by Featherstone, Miss Rigg subsequently married John Raffles, the aforementioned employee of Dunkirk and conspirator with Bulstrode to defraud Will Ladislaw of his inheritance. It will help here to refer to another tree (see Fig. 2).

Thus John Raffles, fence, blackmailer, gambler, the most despicable character in the novel, is related to Casaubon and (by subsequent marriages in the novel) to Lydgate, Dorothea Brooke, Will Ladislaw, and Sir James Chettam. The line of connection goes as follows: Raffles's wife is the mother of Peter Featherstone's child and heir; Peter Featherstone is the husband of Lucy Vincy's sister; Lucy Vincy is the wife of Walter Vincy, the mother of Rosamond (who marries Lydgate) and the sister of Harriet Bulstrode; Harriet is the wife of Nicholas Bulstrode; Bulstrode was the second husband of the former Mrs Dunkirk; Sarah Dunkirk was the wife of Ladislaw Jr.; Ladislaw Jr. was the cousin (by his Aunt Julia) of Edward Casaubon; Casaubon is the husband of Dorothea; Dorothea is the sister-in-law of Sir James Chettam. Put simply, Bulstrode is (by marriage) Casaubon's cousin, Dorothea's cousin, Will's

Figure 1

Casaubon Sr. = Mrs Casaubon – [sister] – Julia [?] = Ladislaw Sr   [Archie] Dunkirk = Mrs Dunkirk [subsequently Mrs Nicholas Bulstrode]

[an older son who dies]   Edward Casaubon   Ladislaw Jr. = Sarah   [a son who dies]

Will Ladislaw

Dorothea Brooke marries, first, Edward Casaubon, then, as the widowed Dorothea Casaubon, Will Ladislaw, by whom she has children

Figure 2

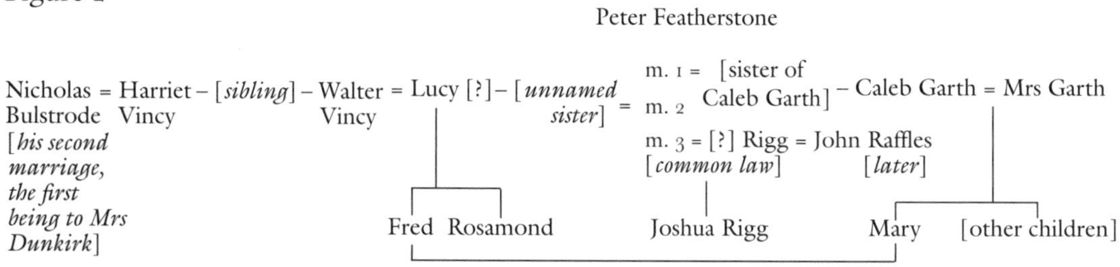

Peter Featherstone

Nicholas = Harriet – [sibling] – Walter = Lucy [?] – [unnamed sister] =   m. 1 = [sister of Caleb Garth] – Caleb Garth = Mrs Garth
Bulstrode Vincy   Vincy   m. 2
[his second marriage, the first being to Mrs Dunkirk]   m. 3 = [?] Rigg = John Raffles [common law] [later]

Fred   Rosamond   Joshua Rigg   Mary   [other children]

Fred Vincy subsequently marries Mary Garth, Rosamond Vincy marries Tertius Lydgate step-grandfather, and related in some way to virtually everyone in the novel.

Every main character in *Middlemarch*'s massive plot can be connected by lines of consanguinity or marriage in this way – with the exception of Farebrother (who none the less regards himself as an 'uncle' to the Garth children). Clearly, it is part of Eliot's grand design, and pertains to what Rosemary Ashton aptly calls, 'the central metaphor of *Middlemarch*, the web'.[1] One of the odd features about the novel, however, is that we are not always sure how aware the main characters are of the webs of kinship that exist between them. This is particularly the case with Casaubon.

We know something of Casaubon's background from incidental remarks. Before their marriage, he tells his fiancée Dorothea that his mother was one of two daughters, just like Dorothea and Celia. Of his father we know nothing, except that Lowick is the family home and Casaubon's mother was a young woman there – whether she had been brought there as a bride, or had lived there as a child, we do not know. Edward was a younger son, and – after ordination – was given the living at Lowick. Subsequently his elder brother died (both parents were evidently already dead at this point) and he came into the manor as well as the vicarage. All these Casaubon deaths must have occurred much earlier, in the narrative's distant prehistory. It was evidently as the head of the family that Ladislaw Jr. approached Edward for help, and this was when Will was still too young to know anything about his circumstances other than that he was very hungry.

In this context one may note a remark which the Revd Cadwallader makes early in the narrative to Sir James Chettam. Sir James, still smarting at the absurd idea that Dorothea, whom he loves, should choose to marry such a dry stick as Casaubon, asks what kind of man he is. 'He is very good to his poor relations,' Cadwallader says, using the plural form of the word.

'he . . . pensions several of the women, and is educating a young fellow [i.e. Will] at a good deal of expense. Casaubon acts up to his sense of justice. His mother's sister made a bad match – a Pole, I think – lost herself – at any rate was disowned by her family. If it had not been for that, Casaubon would not have had so much money by half. *I believe he went himself to find out his cousins*, and see what he could do for them.' [My italics]

We never discover who these unnamed 'relations', 'women', 'cousins' are. They make no appearance at Casaubon's funeral, nor is any bequest to them mentioned in the subsequent lengthy discussion of the will. Dorothea inherits everything, as we understand (Will, who might have expected 'half', is spitefully excluded). What is interesting, however, is Cadwallader's recollection that Casaubon has made active investigations about his relatives, presumably on coming into his inheritance. He would surely have extended his enquiries to his Aunt Julia and her offspring and might even have found out something about the murky world of the Dunkirks.

In conversation with Dorothea shortly after Casaubon's first heart-attack, Will casually tells her that his 'grandmother [was] disinherited because she made what they called a *mésalliance*, though there was nothing to be said against her husband, except that he was a Polish refugee who gave lessons for his bread.' Dorothea goes on to ask what he knew about his parents and grandparents, and Will replies:

'only that my grandfather was a patriot – a bright fellow – could speak many languages – musical – got his bread by teaching all sorts of things. They [i.e. grandfather and grandmother] both died rather early. And I never knew much of my father, beyond what my mother told me; but he inherited the musical talents. I remember his slow walk and his long thin hands; and one day remains with me when he was lying ill, and I was very hungry, and had only a little bit of bread.'

Shortly after, Will recalls, 'My father . . . made himself known to Mr Casaubon and that was my last hungry day.' And shortly after that, his father died.

An initial mystery is why Julia's alliance with a cultivated Pole should have resulted in such a total alienation from her family. A second mystery is Casaubon's extraordinary disinclination to discuss anything to do with Will's origins. He returns all Dorothea's enquiries with 'cold vagueness' and refuses outright to answer any of his wife's questions about 'the mysterious "Aunt Julia" '. Thirdly, one may wonder why Casaubon, an extraordinarily rectitudinous man, does not make over part of the family portion to Will, if he is the legitimate grandson of the older daughter (Julia) who would – had she not made her *mésalliance* – have inherited half or more of her parents' wealth, wealth which has all funnelled into the sole possession of Casaubon.

These questions, particularly the last, should be borne in mind when scrutinising Raffles's account of how, all those years ago, he discovered Will and his mother and kept the news secret from Mrs Dunkirk, at Bulstrode's behest. 'Lord, you made a pretty thing out of me,' Raffles tells Bulstrode, on their reunion at Stone Court: 'and I got but little. I've often thought since, I might have done better by telling the old woman that I'd found her daughter and her grandchild: it would have suited my feelings better.' He goes on, after revealing that Bulstrode gave him enough to emigrate comfortably to America,

'I did have another look after Sarah again, though I didn't tell you; I'd a tender conscience about that pretty young woman. I didn't find her, but I found out her husband's name, and I made a note of it. But hang it, I lost my pocket book. However, if I heard it, I should know it again . . . It began with L; it was almost all l's, I fancy.'

The name, of course, is Ladislaw. This accounts for why it is Bulstrode does not put two and two together when his young step-grandson turns up in Middlemarch. But under what name, then, did Raffles first discover the mother and child? One has to assume he discovered them as 'Sarah and Will Dunkirk'. It beggars credulity that if he were charged to find proof of their identity, with £100,000 at stake, he would not have made some attempt to ascertain names and identities. Without some name to work with, how could he (or his lawyers) have found them in the first place?

This may be taken in conjunction with Ladislaw's extreme sensitivity on the subject of his mother. Consider, for example, Raffles's overture to Will, once he has tumbled to who he is. 'Excuse me, Mr Ladislaw,' he asks:

> 'was your mother's name Sarah Dunkirk?'
>
> Will, starting to his feet, moved backward a step, frowning, and saying with some fierceness, 'Yes, sir, it was. And what is that to you?' . . . 'No offence, my good sir, no offence! I only remember your mother – knew her when she was a girl. But it is your father that you feature, sir. I had the pleasure of seeing your father too. Parents alive, Mr Ladislaw?'
>
> 'No!' thundered Will, in the same attitude as before.

One notes that Raffles does not say – as would be normal – 'Was your mother's maiden name Sarah Dunkirk?' One notes too the extraordinary anger which Raffles's enquiry provokes. The same angry response is evident in Will's interview with the repentant Bulstrode, very shortly after:

> 'I am told that your mother's name was Sarah Dunkirk, and that she ran away from her friends to go on the stage. Also, that your father was at one time much emaciated by illness. May I ask if you can confirm these statements?'

'Yes, they are all true,' said Will . . . 'Do you know any particulars of your mother's family?' [Bulstrode] continued.

'No; she never liked to speak of them. She was a very generous, honourable woman,' said Will, almost angrily.

'I do not wish to allege anything against her . . .'

One notes again the use of the name 'Sarah Dunkirk' rather than, 'your mother's name was Sarah Dunkirk before marriage'. Also prominent is Ladislaw's touchiness at any aspersion against his mother's 'honour'.

There seems at least a prima-facie case for wondering whether or not Will was born out of wedlock. This would explain why it is that he and his mother are first found by Raffles under some other name than Ladislaw (presumably 'Sarah Dunkirk and son'). Irregular unions were common enough in the nineteenth-century theatre world. It is worth recalling too that Will Ladislaw is known to be an idealised portrait of George Eliot's consort, G. H. Lewes. And, as Rosemary Ashton's recent biography has revealed, Lewes was illegitimate.[2] As Ashton notes, Lewes may not himself have known the fact. She adds: 'It is not surprising . . . that we know nothing about G. H. Lewes's earliest years. They must have been precarious socially, and probably financially as well . . . Whatever Lewes was told about his own father . . . he nowhere mentions [him] in his surviving writings.' There is, of course, a difference. It seems that at some point Ladislaw Jr. did marry Sarah Dunkirk – possibly as he felt death was coming, and he needed to hand over responsibility to Casaubon, he made an honest woman of Sarah and a legitimate child out of Will. All this is highly speculative. But any ideas we form about this aspect of the novel are driven to guesswork. One could, of course, speculate that Sarah when she left her parents took on a stage-name, and it was under this that Raffles first found her. There is also the baffling detail that at one point in the narrative Raffles seems to refer to Sarah's family name as 'Duncan'.

One is on firmer ground with hypotheses about what must have been going through Casaubon's mind, and agonising him, as he watched Dorothea and Will forming a close relationship. He may well have known (from his interviews with Ladislaw Jr. and Will's mother, who has been alive until quite recently) about the discreditable 'Jew pawnbroker' business, if only vaguely. Should he tell the young man? Casaubon may also, as I have speculated, have known that Will was born out of wedlock (which would explain why he had not made part of the family fortune over to him, as a legitimate heir). At the very least, it seems strongly probable that Casaubon is possessed of some guilty knowledge and that the anxiety of it hastens his premature death.

What Does Edward Hyde Look Like?

Say 'Jekyll and Hyde', and the person you are speaking to will see in the mind's eye Spencer Tracy's amiably pudgy features dissolving into the monstrous physiognomy of Edward Hyde. The transformation is one of the high points of early Hollywood special effects and close-up camera artistry. The Oxford World's Classics volume pays tribute to the 1941 film by carrying on its cover a still photograph of Tracy in his Hyde makeup. Thanks to the film, when they think of Jekyll and Hyde many modern readers see a face very vividly and in great detail. One of the puzzles in Stevenson's source text, however, is that where Hyde's face ought to be in the narrative there is a blank – rather like the facial features technologically fuzzed out in television documentaries and newscasts 'to protect the innocent'. What precisely was Stevenson's motive for doing this?

The numerous descriptions of Edward Hyde in the narrative agree on a number of points: (1) he is physically small; (2) he is a 'gentleman'; (3) he is young; (4) he is, in some unspecified way, 'deformed'. Jekyll, by contrast, is 'a large, well-made, smooth-faced man of fifty', possessed of a 'large handsome face'. The first eyewitness description which we are given of Hyde arises out of the 3 a.m. outrage when he tramples a little girl in the London street (only children and the very aged are at risk from Edward Hyde, who is not, it seems, inclined to tackle fully grown, physically active adults). According to Mr Enfield, the assailant is 'a little man'. That he is also a 'gentleman' is testified to by his having a bank account at Coutts and his evening dress. Enfield gives no description of the monster's face, but recalls that it was his manner, his 'black sneering coolness', which infuriated the onlookers. Describing the nasty episode to Utterson, Enfield strikes what is to be a recurrent note in response to the question 'What sort of man is he to see?' He is not easy to describe, Enfield recalls:

'There is something wrong with his appearance; something displeasing, something downright detestable. I never saw a man I so disliked, and yet I scarce know why. He must be deformed somewhere; he gives a strong feeling of deformity, although I couldn't specify the point. He's an extraordinary-looking man, and yet I really can name nothing out of the way. No, sir; I can make no hand of it; I can't describe him. And it's not want of memory; for I declare I can see him at this moment.'

Playing the part of 'Mr Seek', Utterson himself comes across Mr Hyde in the streets after one of his horrible nocturnal adventures. The encounter produces the following Identikit picture: 'He was small and very plainly dressed, and the look of him . . . went somehow strongly against the watcher's inclination . . . Mr Hyde was pale and dwarfish, he gave an impression of deformity without any nameable malformation.' Later, arising out of the Carew murder case, the anonymous maidservant who witnessed the crime describes 'a very small gentleman'. This is the best she can do, although she manages a fuller description of Sir Danvers Carew, MP, 'an aged and beautiful gentleman with white hair'. What colour, then, was Hyde's hair? Evidently her eyes are sharp enough to pick up such detail, but something prevents her 'seeing' the assailant. Her identification is exclusively moral: the murderer was 'particularly small and particularly wicked looking'. The chapter ends with another highly charged passage which expatiates on Hyde's inscrutability, his powerful nonentity:

[He] had numbered few familiars . . . his family could nowhere be traced; he had never been photographed; and the few who could describe him differed widely, as common observers will. Only on

one point, were they agreed; and that was the haunting sense
of unexpressed deformity with which the fugitive impressed his
beholders.

It is worth pausing here because, over the last fifty years,
Mr Hyde has been very widely 'photographed' – that is to say,
he has been depicted in innumerable films and television adaptations. These versions of Mr Hyde invariably agree on what
he looks like: simian, excessively hairy, thick-lipped, beetle-
browed, swarthy, middle-aged, and physically massive (see the
Oxford World's Classics cover). One of the 'artist's impres-
sions' loved by newspapers would be very easy to draw up.
None the less, in Stevenson's source narrative Hyde continues
through the middle and later stages shrouded in physical and
physiognomic vagueness. There is, for instance, the strange
episode in which Jekyll's servant sees Edward Hyde in his master's laboratory and assumes that – like the Elephant Man – he
wears 'a mask upon his face'. His subsequent description is as
unhelpful as those of all the other witnesses have been ('When
that masked thing like a monkey jumped from among the
chemicals and whipped into the cabinet, it went down my
spine like ice.') When, in the climax of the melodrama, Dr
Lanyon confronts Edward Hyde face to face, any clear description of the monster is once again withheld:

> Here, at last, I [Lanyon is writing] had a chance of clearly seeing
> him. I had never set eyes on him before, so much was certain. He
> was small, as I have said; I was struck besides with the shocking ex-
> pression of his face, with his remarkable combination of great
> muscular activity and great apparent debility of constitution, and
> – last but not least – with the odd, subjective disturbance caused
> by his neighbourhood.

On his part, looking at the twitching dying visage of Hyde,
Utterson declares, 'The cords of his face still moved with a

semblance of life, but life was quite gone.' All this tells us is that Hyde is possessed of a face. What that face's lineaments or features are we can only guess.

The sum of the physiognomic description which we are given is very unsatisfactory. The only concrete detail we have is that Hyde's face is 'pale', which does not much help the mind's eye picture him. Henry Jekyll's own final testament adds one small detail, which has been eagerly seized on by film-makers. It occurs during an unwilled metamorphosis when, to his horror, Dr Jekyll discovers he has changed personality during a 'comfortable morning doze':

> I was still so engaged when, in one of my more wakeful moments, my eye fell upon my hand. Now the hand of Henry Jekyll (as you have often remarked) was professional in shape and size: it was large, firm, white and comely. But the hand which I now saw, clearly enough, in the yellow light of a mid-London morning, lying half shut on the bed clothes, was lean, corded, knuckly, of a dusky pallor and thickly shaded with a swart growth of hair. It was the hand of Edward Hyde.

Taking this cue, special-effects departments have gone straight for the box marked 'Werewolf'. In the famous Lon Chaney movie, the hero is seen by the technique of stop-frame photography transmuting in front of the camera's eye from respectable middle-class man to disgusting hairy monster. So, too, does Spencer Tracy transmute in the film, *Jekyll and Hyde*. In fact, there is no warrant for assuming a hairy, monstrous Hyde. This is the only reference to hairiness which we are given. There are many more countervailing references in the text to his being 'pale' and 'childlike'. It may well be that a distraught Jekyll is not seeing himself clearly at this point – he may be hallucinating. It is more likely that Hyde now looks different from what he initially did. Jekyll goes on to say in his 'Statement of the Case':

That part of me which I had the power of projecting, had lately been much exercised and nourished; it had seemed to me of late as though the body of Edward Hyde had grown in stature, as though (when I wore that form) I were conscious of a more generous tide of blood . . .

Following the logic of this statement, Mr Hyde should be conceived as changing from young, hairless, juvenile monster in his early manifestations to the hirsute, middle-aged, bulkier monster of his last appearance. No such distinction is traditionally made in film versions. To summarise: there are, it seems, some very good photographs of Mr Hyde – but they are not Stevenson's. In his album there is a perfect blank, apart from the tantalising snapshot of one enigmatic hand.

Is Alec a Rapist?

There has been an interesting slippage in critical discussion of the climax of 'Phase the First' ('The Maiden') of Hardy's *Tess of the d'Urbervilles: A Pure Woman* over the last century. Victorian critics, to a man and woman, assume that the luckless maiden is at least partly the author of her own misfortune. As Mowbray Morris put it in the *Quarterly Review* (April 1892):

> For the first half of his story the reader may indeed conceive it to have been Mr Hardy's design to show how a woman essentially honest and pure at heart will, through the adverse shocks of fate, eventually rise to higher things. But if this were his original purpose he must have forgotten it before his tale was told, or perhaps the 'true sequence of things' was too strong for him. For what are the higher things to which this poor creature eventually rises? She rises through seduction to adultery, murder and the gallows.[1]

Writing a month earlier in *Blackwood's Magazine*, Mrs Oliphant is fierce against Tess for not having withstood temptation better:

> We have not a word to say against the force and passion of this story. It is far finer in our opinion than anything Mr Hardy has ever done before. The character of Tess up to her last downfall . . . is consistent enough, and we do not object to the defiant blazon of a Pure Woman, notwithstanding the early stain. But a Pure Woman is not betrayed into fine living and fine clothes as the mistress of her seducer by any stress of poverty or misery; and Tess

was a skilled labourer, for whom it is very rare that nothing can be found to do. Here the elaborate and indignant plea for Vice, that it is really Virtue, breaks down altogether.[2]

Morris and Oliphant take it for granted that Tess was 'seduced' – that is, led astray, not violated or forced into sexual intercourse against her will. Compare this Victorian view with the downrightness of Tony Tanner, writing in 1968:

> Hardy's vision is tragic and penetrates far deeper than specific social anomalies. One is more inclined to think of Sophocles than, say, Zola, when reading Hardy . . . Tess is the living demonstration of these tragic ironies. That is why she who is raped lives to be hanged.[3]

She who was seduced in 1892 is she who is raped in the permissive 1960s. Even those modern commentators unwilling to go the whole way hedge their bets. Thus, the first edition of the *Oxford Companion to English Literature* (1932) declares 'Tess is seduced.' Margaret Drabble's fifth edition of *OCEL* (1984), while retaining the substance of the *Tess* entry, states 'Tess is cunningly seduced.' The 1993 literary encyclopaedia *The 1890s* backs both horses by opening its *Tess* entry with the statement: 'This simple story of seduction-cum-rape', and goes on to describe what happens in the Chase as 'virtual rape'.[4] Ian Gregor, in his influential study of Hardy's major novels, goes all the way by declaring that 'it is both a seduction *and* a rape' (try that in court).[5] The Oxford World's Classics edition's editors, Juliet Grindle and Simon Gatrell, use the ambiguous term 'betrayed' (as does OUP's blurb-writer) and the non-felonious 'violated' ('violation' will not land you with a ten-year prison term, 'rape' will). Writing in the 1990s, with the complexities of 'date rape' hovering in the air, James Gibson refers edgily to Tess's 'sexual molestation by Alec' and his 'sexual harassment of his victim'. In his outline of

the crucial episode in the 'Text Summary' section of the Everyman edition, Gibson reverts to a more Tannerian reading of events:

Chapter 11

Alec rides with Tess into the Chase – works on her by appearing to be worried about her safety and emphasising the presents he has sent to her family – he deliberately loses the way – after pretending to go in search of the way he returns and rapes her.[6]

So what does happen in the Chase on that September night – seduction, cunning seduction, betrayal, sexual molestation, sexual harassment, violation, 'virtual rape', or rape? The first point to note is that Hardy himself was somewhat unsure about the 'naughty chapters' (as Mrs Oliphant called them). In the serialisation of the story in the *Graphic* newspaper (July–December 1891) he was prevailed on by nervous editors to drop the Chaseborough dance and subsequent seduction/rape sequence altogether, putting in its place an entirely new sub-plot. In the *Graphic* version of *Tess*, the heroine is tricked into a fake marriage, and is thus deflowered with her full (if de-luded) consent. This venerable device had been used earlier by Charles Reade in *Put Yourself in His Place* (1870), by Thack-eray in *Philip* (1862), and, aboriginally, by Scott in *St Ronan's Well* (1823). The attraction of the bogus-marriage gimmick was that it enabled the hoodwinked heroine to commit the act of fornication innocently, thus preserving her 'purity'. In the three-volume edition, which came out in November 1891, Hardy repudiated artifice and insisted on reprinting the ori-ginal rape/seduction text, with the prefatory proclamation: 'If an offence come out of the truth, better is it that the offence come than that the truth be concealed.'

Even in the frank versions of 'The Maiden', however, much is left inscrutable, if not entirely concealed. The rape/seduc-tion episode begins with a description of the Trantridge peas-antry's loose morals and hard drinking, which are given free rein in their Saturday-night festivities at the nearby 'decayed market-town', Chaseborough. Tess, we are told, likes to go to these Saturday-night affairs, although she does not participate in the revelry. On the misty September Saturday night in ques-tion, Tess makes her way from Chaseborough to a barn in a nearby 'townlet' where her fellow Trantridge cottagers are at a 'private jig'. She wants their company on the way home, since there has been both a fair and a market-day at Chaseborough, and there may be drunken men in the country lanes. When she arrives at the dance, Tess discovers a surreal scene. The barn floor is deep in 'scroff' – 'that is to say the powdery residuum from the storage of peat and other products, the stir-ring of which by [the dancers'] turbulent feet created [a] neb-ulosity that involved the scene . . . [a] floating, fusty *débris* of peat and hay'. The dusty haze thrown up by the dancers' muffled stamping merges with the mist, and later the fog, which enshrouds the whole of the seduction/rape episode in a corresponding moral 'nebulosity'.

The dustily indistinct picture of the dance has been connected with the pictorial influence of French Impressionism on Hardy and is one of his fine visual set-pieces. At a more physical level, the scene alludes to a common belief in country communities – that flying dust, as it gets trapped in their underwear, has a sexually exciting effect on women dancers. It is part of the folklore of barn-dances in America that unscrupulous young men – intending to induce wantonness in their partners – scatter pepper on the boards before the evening gets under way. Certainly the 'scroff' seems to have had an aphrodisiac effect at Chaseborough. Hardy hints at sexual orgy by a string of meaningful classical references:

> They coughed as they danced, and laughed as they coughed. Of the rushing couples there could barely be discerned more than the high lights – the indistinctness shaping them to satyrs clasping nymphs – a multiplicity of Pans whirling a multiplicity of Syrinxes; Lotis attempting to elude Priapus, and always failing.

Each of these three allusions signals 'rape'. Tess is invited to join in by a dusty, sweating swain. But she refuses. She becomes aware of the glowing tip of Alec's cigar in the gloom behind her. He offers to take her home, but although she is very tired she declines, not quite trusting him – perhaps forewarned by the phallic heat of his Havana on her neck. But later, when Car Darch (one of Alec's cast-off mistresses) threatens violence, Tess allows herself (a maiden in distress) to be rescued by Alec, now on horseback. This is the prelude to Chapter 11. Chaseborough is only three miles from Trantridge, and the journey on Alec's stallion should take twenty minutes or so. But he deliberately loses his way, turning his horse into the foggy wilderness of the Chase – 'the oldest wood in England'. Tess, who has been up since five every day that week, is exhausted. As she falls asleep in the saddle, Alec puts his arm around her waist. 'This immediately put her on the defensive,' we are told, 'and with one of those sudden impulses of reprisal to which she was liable she gave him a little push from her.' Alec almost tumbles off the horse. It is a significant detail. The push looks forward to Tess's eventually stabbing Alec to death, which – we apprehend – is another reflexive 'impulse of reprisal'. Here it stresses that even when her body is dormant, Tess's purity is vigilant and well capable of defending itself. This is important, since she will be sleeping when the seduction/rape occurs.

The point is also stressed that Alec has not directed his horse's head into the Chase with any overtly mischievous intention, but merely 'to prolong companionship with her'. Tess repulses his love-making as they ride, without ever distinctly denying that she loves him. He is much encouraged by her lack of 'frigidity'. He contrives further to weaken her resolve with the information that he has bought her father a new horse, to replace the luckless Prince, who died as a result of her falling asleep on the road. Once again, it seems that Tess is falling into dangerous slumber. Alec, who by now is completely lost in the fog and trees, wraps her in his coat, makes a 'sort of couch or nest' for her in the newly dropped leaves, and goes off on foot to look for some landmark. He eventually locates the road, and returns to find Tess fast asleep. He bends down to her, 'till her breath warmed his face, and in a moment his cheek was in contact with hers. She was sleeping soundly, and upon her eyelashes there lingered tears'.

This is the last image Hardy leaves us with. It could be Prince Charming about to wake Sleeping Beauty, or it could be ravishing Tarquin. The narrative averts its gaze from whatever happens next and moralises loftily for three paragraphs. The clearest clue as to what is meanwhile going on between Tess and Alec is given in the second of these paragraphs:

Why it was that upon this beautiful feminine tissue, sensitive as gossamer, and practically blank as snow as yet, there should have been traced such a coarse pattern as it was doomed to receive; why so often the coarse appropriates the finer thus, the wrong man the woman, the wrong woman the man, many thousand years of analytical philosophy have failed to explain to our sense of order. One may, indeed, admit the possibility of a retribution lurking in the present catastrophe. Doubtless some of Tess d'Urberville's mailed ancestors rollicking home from a fray had dealt the same measure even more ruthlessly towards peasant girls of their time. But though to visit the sins of the fathers upon the children may be a morality good enough for divinities, it is scorned by average human nature; and it therefore does not mend the matter.

As Thackeray says in *Vanity Fair*, the novelist knows everything. Hardy must know what is going on here, even if he chooses not to tell us. Clearly intercourse is taking place while the narrator turns away and prates about olden times. But what kind of intercourse? All the narrative divulges to the reader is that Alec is not as 'ruthless' as those ancient ravishers, Tess's ancestors, taking their seigneurial rights. It is clear that Alec has not set out with the explicit purpose of assaulting Tess; when he leaves her in her leafy couch, it is genuinely to find the road home, not to lull her into defencelessness. Not that she would normally be defenceless. The point is made earlier in the chapter that even when asleep, Tess is able to fend off unwanted sexual advances. Why does she not protect her imperilled virtue with one of those timely 'impulses of reprisal'?

More significantly, when – a maiden no more – Tess upbraids Alec, she does not accuse him of rape, but of having duped her: 'I didn't understand your meaning till it was too late,' she says. Nor, when upbraiding her mother for not warning her against men, does Tess claim that she has been raped. As the narrative glosses her thoughts:

> She had never wholly cared for [Alec], she did not at all care for
> him now. She had dreaded him, winced before him, succumbed
> to adroit advantages he took of her helplessness; then, temporar-
> ily blinded by his ardent manners, had been stirred to confused
> surrender awhile: had suddenly despised and disliked him, and
> had run away.

Alec, we understand, has been 'adroit' – some cunning caresses
with his hands are implied. His 'ardent manners' (an odd
conjunction – ardour is rarely well mannered) had 'stirred'
Tess – erection is hinted at. The verb 'stirred' is significant,
suggesting as it does physical reciprocation on Tess's part. Did
she consent? 'Confused surrender' suggests that she did, but
that she was blinded at the time by his stimulating foreplay
and the power of her own aroused feelings.

  . By Victorian legal lights it was clearly seduction; there was
nothing forcible in Alec's actions, although, as he himself
avows ('I did wrong – I admit it'), they were the actions of a
cad. He 'took advantage' of her. This is immoral, but not criminal. Even by the strict 21st-century definition of rape on North
American campuses, his behaviour would probably not be
criminal. It is not recorded that Tess clearly told Alec to stop,
once he had started to make love to her. 'Stirred' as she was,
she may well have encouraged him to continue making love by
body movements of her own. That is, neither seduction nor
rape may be the proper term; Tess was a willing, if misguided,
participant in her own undoing.

  Why then do modern critics and readers assume that Alec
is a rapist? For the same reason that they are unwilling to see
Tess as a murderess. Here again, Hardy manipulates our response in his heroine's favour less by what he describes than by
what he omits to describe. To summarise: hearing unusual
'sounds', Mrs Brooks, the landlady at the Herons, the inn
where Alec and Tess have taken an apartment, looks through
the keyhole. She sees Tess in distress at the breakfast-table, and

hears a long complaint ('a dirge rather than a soliloquy') from her lips. Tess is berating herself for her weakness in surrendering again to Alec's 'cruel persuasions'. She sees herself as an irredeemably fallen adulteress. Mrs Brooks hears 'more and sharper words from the man', then 'a sudden rustle'. Tess soon after hurries away from the inn, dressed in black. Alec's body is discovered on the bed, stabbed through the heart.

Tess's subsequent explanation to Angel is not entirely satisfactory.

> 'But how do you mean – you have killed him?'
>
>   'I mean that I have,' she murmured in a reverie.
>
> 'What – bodily? Is he dead?'
>
>   'Yes. He heard me crying about you, and he bitterly taunted me; and called you by a foul name; and then I did it; my heart could not bear it: he had nagged me about you before – and then I dressed myself, and came away to find you.'

Hardy does not give us any details of the subsequent trial, leaping straight from Tess, arrested on the sacrificial slab at Stonehenge, to her execution at Wintoncester Gaol. But it would be interesting to know what came out in court. By Mrs Brooks's testimony (as we have it), it would seem that Alec – justifiably vexed by Tess's long diatribe against himself – said something 'sharp' ('bitterly taunted' seems an overstatement). It is hard to think up a 'foul name' applicable to a man ('no-balls eunuch'?) which would justify what followed. Tess then picked up the carving-knife from the breakfast-table, walked all the way across the length of the living-room to the bed on which Alec was still lying, and stabbed him through the heart. One precisely aimed stroke has killed him. It is hard to imagine how this could be done – given Alec's superior strength and agility – unless Tess waited until he relapsed into sleep, as people do before breakfast. An awake Alec would hardly watch Tess stalking towards him with an upraised knife without raising a hand to defend himself or shifting his torso away from the path of the murder weapon.

It is conceivable that a legal defence could be made for Tess along the lines that lawyers successfully defended Lorena Bobbit – the aggrieved Virginian who cut off her husband's penis with a carving-knife while he slept. Possibly a contemporary jury might acquit Tess, on the grounds that she, like Lorena, had suffered years of abuse from her partner (although Alec is not recorded as ever striking or beating Tess). But the jury would not, one imagines, acquit her as readily and absolutely as do the literary critics. This, for instance, is how James Gibson summarises the climactic chapter:

Chapter 56

The landlady of the lodging-house is curious – hears Tess moaning in her room and sharp words – she sees Tess leaving the house and then a red spot on the ceiling – Alec is dead.[7]

'Alec is murdered' would seem to be truer to the facts. Hardy's rhetoric allows the critic to overlook the simple wrongness of Tess's act, and mask it in a neutral phraseology more appropriate to suicide or death by natural causes than homicide. The holes in Hardy's account allow us to jump to conclusions ('Alec is a rapist who gets what is coming to him') and sanction such exonerating imagery as Tony Tanner's: 'Tess is gradually crucified on the oppugnant ironies of circumstance and existence itself.' On objective legal grounds, one might retort, Tess deserves crucifixion rather more than do the two thieves and their famous companion. It would be much harder to sustain the 'Tess as Christ figure' line if readers had before them a clear image of her plunging the carving-knife into Alec's sleeping body, choosing her spot carefully so as to kill him with one blow – all because he had applied some unspecified 'foul name' to her husband. Nor would it be easy, I imagine, to sustain the 'Tess as a victim of rape' line (which leads directly into the 'justifiable homicide' line) if one had a clear image of her making reciprocal love to Alec in the Chase. Hardy's novel is like a court-case in which all the material evidence is left out, and the jury (readers) rushed to judgment on the basis of the defendant's beauty and pathetic suffering alone.

All this is not to suggest that Tess is a murderous slut who gets what is coming to her. But one should perhaps give more credence to Mrs Oliphant's Victorian common-sensical view. Alec is not a rapist and, although her innocence makes her vulnerable, Tess must take some small responsibility for what happens in the Chase. Tess does have a saleable skill, and she did not have to surrender a second time to Alec purely for economic reasons. Nor, having surrendered, did she have to compound adultery with wilful murder. Had Hardy, in the manner of some Victorian John Grisham, supplied us with two closely described trials in the body of the novel (the first of Alec for rape, the second of Tess for murder), our verdict would surely be harder on Tess, and lighter on Alec.

Why Is Griffin Cold?

H. G. Wells was keen that his 'scientific romances' should be just that – scientific. He devotes a whole section of *The Invisible Man* (Chapter 19, 'Certain First Principles') to authentication of the central concept in the novel. It is, for the lay-reader at least, an extraordinarily plausible performance. 'Have you already forgotten your physics?' Griffin asks his old classmate, Kemp, before launching into a lecture on optics:

> 'Just think of all the things that are transparent and seem not to be so. Paper, for instance, is made up of transparent fibres, and it is white and opaque only for the same reason that a powder of glass is white and opaque. Oil white paper, fill up the interstices between the particles with oil so that there is no longer refraction or reflection except at the surfaces, and it becomes as transparent as glass. And not only paper, but cotton fibre, linen fibre, woody fibre, and *bone*, Kemp, *flesh*, Kemp, *hair*, Kemp, *nails* and *nerves*, Kemp, in fact the whole fabric of a man except the red of his blood and black pigment of hair, are all made up of transparent, colourless tissue. So little suffices to make us visible one to the other. For the most part the fibres of a living creature are no more opaque than water.'

'Of course, of course,' responds Kemp, suddenly remembering his undergraduate physics, 'I was thinking only last night of the sea larvae and all jelly-fish!'

Wells managed to finesse the business about the black pigment in hair by making Griffin albino. But one feature of his invisibility hypothesis continued to bother the author, and evidently remained insolubly inauthentic.

As he later explained in a letter to Arnold Bennett:

> Any alteration of the refractive index of the eye lenses would make vision impossible. Without such alteration the eyes would be visible as glassy globules. And for vision it is also necessary that there should be visual purple behind the retina and an opaque cornea and iris. On these lines you would get a very effective short story but nothing more.[1]

There are other irrationalities flawing the central conception of *The Invisible Man* which Wells seems not to have commented on. The most memorable episode in the novel is Griffin's recollection to Kemp of how, newly invisible in London, he discovered himself not omnipotent (as he fondly expected) but more wretched than the most destitute of street beggars, wholly impotent, a modern version of Lear's poor forked animal:

> 'But you begin to realise now', said the Invisible Man, 'the full disadvantage of my condition. I had no shelter, no covering. To get clothing was to forgo all my advantage, to make of myself a strange and terrible thing. I was fasting; for to eat, to fill myself with unassimilated matter, would be to become grotesquely visible again.'

This sticks indelibly in the mind. Like Midas, Griffin's dream of vast power turns to a terrible curse. It is January. What more distressing than to be naked and starving in the cold streets?

And yet, if we think about it, Griffin could have been as comfortably covered and as well fed as any of his visible fellow-Londoners. As he tells Kemp, describing his first experiments, he discovered early on that any fibre, vegetable, or woody matter can be rendered invisible – particularly if it has not been dyed or stained.[2] Griffin proves this in his earliest experimental trials:

'I needed two little dynamos, and these I worked with a cheap gas engine. My first experiment was with a bit of white wool fabric. It was the strangest thing in the world to see it in the flicker of the flashes soft and white, and then to watch it fade like a wreath of smoke and vanish.'

Griffin moves on to his neighbour's white cat, and the white pillow on which the animal's drugged body is lying – both of which are rendered invisible by his little gas-powered machine.

It is clear that, with a little forethought, Griffin could quite easily make himself an invisible white suit of clothing. He could also render food invisible before eating it, so that its undigested mass did not show up in his otherwise transparent entrails. He could, if he were patient enough, construct himself an invisible house out of invisible wood. If, due to the invasions of suspicious neighbours, he had no time to do this in London, he might certainly do it during his many weeks at Iping (where, as he tells Kemp, most of his efforts seem to be vainly directed towards finding a chemical formula which will enable him to be visible or invisible at will).

The naked, starving, unhoused Griffin would, logically, seem to be that way not because of any fatal flaw in his science. He could, as has been said, walk around in an invisible three-piece suit, with an invisible top hat on his invisible head, an invisible umbrella to keep himself dry, and an invisible three-course meal in his belly. That he does not avail himself of these amenities may, conceivably, be ascribed to a mental derangement provoked by the excruciating pain of the long dematerialisation process.

'I had not expected the suffering. A night of racking anguish, sickness and fainting. I set my teeth, though my skin was presently afire; all my body afire; but I lay there like grim death. I understood now how it was the cat had howled until I chloroformed it.

Lucky it was I lived alone and untended in my room. There were times when I sobbed and groaned and talked. But I stuck to it. I became insensible and woke languid in the darkness.'

But, closely examined, Griffin's derangement seems to originate in the condition of his life well before his agonising passage into invisibility. His aggrieved sense of alienation evidently began early, probably with the bullying and jeers he attracted as a child, on account of his physical abnormality. It is his physical repulsiveness that strikes those who remember him as an adult. Kemp recalls Griffin at University College as 'a younger student, almost an albino, six feet high, and broad, with a pink and white face and red eyes – who won the medal for chemistry'. This evidently was six or seven years since. In his last years as a student, and in his first employment as a lecturer in an unfashionable provincial university, Griffin (who, one guesses, has neither men nor women friends) has deteriorated into a condition of clear paranoia:

'I kept it [i.e. his discovery] to myself. I had to do my work under frightful disadvantages. Oliver, my professor, was a scientific bounder, a journalist by instinct, a thief of ideas, – he was always prying! And you know the knavish system of the scientific world. I simply would not publish, and let him share my credit. I went on working. I got nearer and nearer making my formula into an experiment, a reality. I told no living soul, because I meant to flash my work upon the world with crushing effect, – to become famous at a blow . . . To do such a thing would be to transcend magic. And I beheld, unclouded by doubt, a magnificent vision of all that invisibility might mean to a man, – the mystery, the power, the freedom. Drawbacks I saw none. You have only to think! And I, a shabby, poverty-struck, hemmed-in demonstrator, teaching fools in a provincial college, might suddenly become – this.'

Griffin, in his maniac delusions of divine superiority, despises humanity. When, therefore, he goes among the London crowds naked and starving it is because, like the self-divested Lear on the heath, he is deliberately refusing to wear the uniform of his herd-like fellow man. He has chosen to strip himself. Nakedness is the sign of his difference, and his godlike superiority over the lesser, visible beings he despises. He no more needs trousers than Jove or Satan. It is beneath his notice to concern himself with such minutiae.

Why the 'Single Print of a Foot'?

J. Donald Crowley is amusingly exasperated about Defoe's many narrative delinquencies in *Robinson Crusoe*. 'Perhaps the most glaring lapse', Crowley says in his Oxford World's Classics edition of the novel,

> occurs when Defoe, having announced that Crusoe had pulled off all his clothes to swim out to the shipwreck, has him stuff his pockets with biscuit some twenty lines later. Likewise, for the purpose of creating a realistic effect, he arranges for Crusoe to give up tallying his daily journal because his ink supply is dangerously low; but there is ink aplenty, when, almost twenty-seven years later, Crusoe wants to draw up a contract . . . Having tried to suggest that Crusoe suffers hardship because he lacks salt, he later grants Crusoe the salt in order to illustrate his patient efforts to teach Friday to eat salted meat. Crusoe pens a kid identified as a young male only to have it turn into a female when he hits upon the notion of breeding more of the animals.

Such inconsistencies convince Crowley that 'Defoe wrote too hastily to control his materials completely'. His was a careless genius.

Haste and carelessness could well account for some baffling features in the famous 'discovery of the footprint' scene. It occurs fifteen years into Robinson's occupation of his now thoroughly colonised and (as he fondly thinks) desert island. At this belated point the hero is made to describe his outdoor garb. He has long since worn out the European clothes which survived the wreck. Now his coverings are home-made:

> I had a short Jacket of Goat-Skin, the Skirts coming down
> to about the middle of my Thighs; and a Pair of open-knee'd
> Breeches of the same, the Breeches were made of the Skin of an
> old *He-goat*, whose Hair hung down such a Length on either Side,
> that like *Pantaloons* it reach'd to the middle of my Legs; Stockings
> and Shoes I had none, but had made me a Pair of somethings, I
> scarce know what to call them, like Buskins to flap over my Legs,
> and lace on either Side like Spatter-dashes; but of a most barbarous
> Shape, as indeed were all the rest of my Cloaths.

This sartorial inventory has been gratefully seized on by the
novel's many illustrators, from 1719 onwards. The salient feature is that Robinson goes barefoot. And it is to rivet this detail ('Shoes I had none') in our mind that at this point Defoe
describes Crusoe's wardrobe. In the preceding narrative, if it
crosses the reader's mind, we assume that Crusoe has some
protection for the soles of his feet (the island is a rough place).
Oddly, Robinson seems not to have taken a supply of footwear
from the ship's store nor any cobbling materials with which
to make laced moccasins from goatskin. Shortly after being
marooned he found 'two shoes' washed up on the strand, but
they 'were not fellows', and were of no use to him. Much later,
during his 'last year on the Island', Robinson scavenges a couple of pairs of shoes from the bodies of drowned sailors in the
wreck of the Spanish boat. But, when he sees the naked footprint on the sand, Crusoe is barefoot.

The footprint is epochal, 'a new Scene of my Life', as Crusoe calls it. He has several habitations on the island (his 'estate',
as he likes to think it) and the discovery comes as he walks
from one of his inland residences to the place on the shore
where he has beached his 'boat' (in fact, a primitive canoe):

> It happen'd one Day about Noon going towards my Boat, I was
> exceedingly surpriz'd with the Print of a Man's naked Foot on the
> Shore, which was very plain to be seen in the Sand: I stood like

one Thunder-struck, or as if I had seen an Apparition; I listen'd, I look'd round me, I could hear nothing, nor see any Thing. I went up to a rising Ground to look farther, I went up the Shore and down the Shore, but it was all one, I could see no other Impression but that one, I went to it again to see if there were any more, and observe if it might not be my Fancy; but there was no Room for that, for there was exactly the very Print of a Foot, Toes, Heel, and every Part of a Foot; how it came thither, I knew not, nor could in the least imagine.

Two big questions hang over this episode. The first, most urgent for Robinson, is 'Who made this footprint?' The second, most perplexing for the reader, is 'Why is there only one footprint?' In the above passage, and later, Crusoe is emphatic on the point. We are not much helped by illustrations of the scene, such as that by Lynton Lamb to an early Oxford World's Classics edition, which shows the footprint, on a flat expanse of beach, with nothing else for yards around. (It's a lovely picture, but Lamb has erroneously given Crusoe a pair of Scholl sandals.)

Was the single footprint made by some monstrous hopping cannibal? Perhaps Long John Silver passed by, from *Treasure Island*, with just the one foot and a peg leg? Has someone played a prank on Robinson Crusoe by raking over the sand as one does in a long-jump pit, leaving just the one ominous mark? More seriously, one might surmise that the ground is stony with only a few patches of sand between to receive an occasional footprint. This is the interpretation of G. H. Thomas in his illustrated version of this scene (which features the shoes, again). The objection to the thesis of this illustration is that Crusoe would scarcely choose such a rocky inlet as a convenient place to beach his boat.

Robinson has no time for investigation of the footprint. He retreats in hurried panic to his 'Castle', not emerging for three days. Is it the mark of the devil, he wonders, as he

cowers inside his dark cave? That would explain the supernat-
ural singularity of the footprint, since the devil can fly. In his
fever vision, years before, Robinson saw the Evil One 'descend
from a great black Cloud, in a bright Flame of Fire, and light
upon the Ground' presumably leaving an enigmatic footprint
in the process, if anyone dared look. But if the mark in the
sand is the devil's work it would seem lacking in infernal cunning or even clear purpose: 'The Devil might have found an
abundance of other Ways to have terrify'd me than this of the
single Print of a Foot,' Robinson concludes. Similar arguments
weigh against the footprint's being a sign from the Almighty.
It is more plausible, Robinson finally concludes, 'that it must
be some of the Savages of the main Land over-against me, who
had wander'd out to Sea in their *Canoes*'. Will they now come
back in force, to 'devour' him?

Fear banishes 'all my religious Hope' for a while. But
gradually Crusoe's faith in Providence returns, as does his trust
in rational explanation. 'I began to perswade my self it was all
a Delusion; that it was nothing else but . . . the Print of my
own foot.' He emerges from his hole and, stopping only to
milk the distended teats of his goats, he returns to examine
the print more carefully. In three days and nights one might
expect it to have been covered over by the wind, but it is still
there, clear as ever. Crusoe's rational explanation proves to
be wrong: 'When I came to measure the Mark with my own
Foot, I found my Foot not so large by a great deal.' Panic once
more.

We are never specifically told who left the print, nor why
it was just the one. But the experience changes Robinson
Crusoe's way of life. No longer supposing himself alone, he
adopts a more defensive ('prudent') way of life. He is right
to be prudent. Some two years later, on the other side of
the island, he sees a boat out at sea. That far coast, he now
realises, is frequently visited – unlike his own: 'I was presently
convinc'd, that the seeing the Print of a Man's Foot, was not

such a strange Thing in the Island as I imagin'd.' Providence, he is grateful to realise, has cast him 'upon the Side of the Island, where the Savages never came'. Never? Who left the print then – friendly Providence, as a warning that there were savages about?

Gradually Crusoe comes, by prudent anthropological observation, to know more about the Savages – a process that culminates ten years after the footprint episode with the acquisition of his most valuable piece of property, Man Friday. The savages are, as Robinson observes, opportunist raiders of the sea – black pirates with a taste for human flesh. When they find some luckless wrecked mariner, or defenceless fellow

native in his craft, the savages bring their prey to shore to cook and eat them. Then they leave. In their grisly visits they never penetrate beyond the sandy beach to the interior of the island (perhaps, as in Golding's *Lord of the Flies*, there are legends of a terrible giant, dressed in animal skins, with a magical tube which spurts thunder). It is likely that the footprint must have been left by some scouting savage making a rare foray to the far side of the island. He noticed Crusoe's boat, concluded on close inspection that it was flotsam, and went off again. Luckily the hero's residences, livestock, and plantations were some way distant and could not be seen from this section of the shore.

But why the single footprint? Before attempting an answer one needs to make the point that, although careless in accidental details (such as the trousers and the biscuits), Defoe usually handles substantial twists of plot very neatly. A good example is the corn which Crusoe first thinks is providential manna but which later proves to have a rational origin. Defoe sets this episode up by mentioning that Robinson brought back some barley-seed from his wrecked ship, 'but to my great Disappointment, I found afterwards that the Rats had eaten or spoil'd it all.' He threw it away in disgust. Then, twenty-eight pages later, the seed sprouts. Robinson at first believes the growing barley to be a miracle. Then he puts two and two together and realises it is the result of his thoughtlessly shaking out the bags of spoiled chickenfeed some months earlier. It is an accomplished piece of narrative.

A few pages before the episode of the footprint Defoe has Crusoe describe, in great detail, the tides which wash the island and their intricate ebbs and flows. Many readers will skip over this technical and unexciting digression. Ostensibly, Crusoe's meditation on the 'Sets of the Tides' has to do with navigation problems. But the ulterior motive, we may assume, is to imprint in the reader's mind the fact that the island does have tides and that they are forever lapping at its shoreline.

What we may suppose happened is the following. Crusoe has beached his boat, not on the dead-flat expanse which Lamb portrays, but on a steeply inclined beach. The unknown savage came head-on into the beach and pulled his boat on to the sand. He investigated Crusoe's canoe, all the while walking below the high-tide line. Having satisfied himself that Crusoe's vessel had no one in it, he returned to his own craft. Coming or going, one of his feet (as he was knocked by a wave, perhaps, or jumped away from some driftwood) strayed above the high-water mark. This lateral footprint (i.e. not pointing to, or away from, the ocean) was left after the tide had washed all the others away together with the drag marks of the savage's boat.

Robinson Crusoe's discovery of the footprint is, with Oliver Twist's asking for more, one of the best-known episodes in British fiction – familiar even to those who would scarcely recognise the name of Daniel Defoe. It is also one of the English novel's most illustrated scenes – particularly in the myriad boys' editions of *Robinson Crusoe*. Most illustrations I have seen make one of three errors (as does Lamb in his aforementioned depiction): they put the footprint too far from the waves; they picture Robinson as wearing shoes; they show the beach as too flat. These errors, I think, reflect widespread perplexity at the scene and a fatalistic inclination not to worry too much about its illogical details. But there are, as I have tried to argue, ways of making sense of the single footprint.

Can Jane Eyre Be Happy?

Margaret Smith's introduction to the Oxford World's Classics edition of *Jane Eyre* summarises the formative influence of Charlotte Brontë's reading in the Bible, Bunyan, Shakespeare, Scott, and Wordsworth. Smith expertly identifies the Byronic and Miltonic elements which fuse into the mighty conception of Edward Fairfax Rochester. There is, however, a principal source for *Jane Eyre* which Smith does not mention – a 'fairy story' which, one assumes, was read by or to the Brontë children in their nursery years.

The story of Bluebeard ('*Barbe Bleue*') was given its authoritative literary form in Charles Perrault's *Histoires et Contes du temps passé* (1697). Perrault's fables were much reprinted and adapted by the Victorians into children's picture-books, burlesque, and pantomime. By the 1840s the story of the bad man who locked his superfluous wives in his attic would have been among the best known of fables. In the twentieth century the Bluebeard story, with its savagely misogynistic overtones, has fallen into disfavour. It survives as the source (sometimes unrecognised) for such adult productions as Maeterlinck's play, *Ariane et Barbe Bleue* (1901), Béla Bartok's *Duke Bluebeard's Castle* (1911), John Fowles's *The Collector* (1963), and Margaret Atwood's *Lady Oracle* (1976).[1] Among its other distinctions, *Jane Eyre* can claim to be the first adult, non-burlesque treatment of the Bluebeard theme in English literature.

Perrault's 'Bluebeard' is the story of a rich, middle-aged gentleman, named for his swarthy chin and saturnine manner, who marries a young woman. They take up residence in his country castle. Mr Bluebeard leaves on a trip, giving his wife the keys to the house with a strict instruction not to go to 'the small room at the end of the long passage on the lower floor'. The wife's curiosity is piqued and she disobeys his instruction. In the little room she finds the butchered corpses of Blue-beard's previous wives. In her shock, she drops the key into a pool of blood. On his return Bluebeard sees the stain on the key and deduces what has happened. She must die too, he declares. She is saved in the nick of time by her brothers, who ride to her rescue. They kill Bluebeard and enrich his young widow with her former husband's possessions.

The echoes of 'Bluebeard' in *Jane Eyre* are obvious. Rochester is a swarthy, middle-aged, rich country gentleman, with a wife locked up in a secret chamber in his house. He wants another wife – like Bluebeard, he is a man of voracious sexual appetite. Bertha is 'saved', after a fashion, by her brother. Ingenuity can find numerous other parallels. But what is most striking is Brontë's inversion of the conclusion of the fable. In *Jane Eyre* we are encouraged, in the last chapters, to feel sympathy for Bluebeard – a husband more sinned against than sinning. The locked-up wife is transformed into the villain of the piece. It is as if one were to rewrite 'Little Red Riding Hood' so as to generate sympathy for the wolf, or 'Jack and the Beanstalk' to generate sympathy for the giant who grinds Englishmen's bones to make his bread.

Not only is sympathy demanded. We are to assume that – after some moral re-education – Jane will be blissfully happy with a Bluebeard who has wholly mended his ways. It is the more daring since (putting to one side the intent to commit bigamy), Edward Rochester is responsible for Bertha Rochester's death. Although he claims that 'indirect assassination' is not in his nature, this is exactly how he disposes of his superfluous first wife. Why did he not place her in one of the 'non-restraint' institutions which were transforming treatment of the insane in England in the late 1830s? The York Retreat (where Grace Poole and her son previously worked, we gather) and John Conolly's Hanwell Asylum in Middlesex were achieving remarkable results by *not* immuring patients in 'goblin cells' but allowing them a normal social existence within humanely supervised environments. Bertha Mason, we learn, has lucid spells which sometimes last for weeks. In squalid, solitary confinement, with only Grace Poole as her wardress, what wonder that she relapses? Why, one may ask, does Rochester not put his wife into professional care? Lest in one of her lucid spells she divulges whose wife she is. What 'care' does he provide for her? An alcoholic crone, a diet of porridge, and a garret. And then there is the business of Bertha's actual death, as related by the innkeeper at the Rochester Arms: 'I witnessed, and several more witnessed Mr Rochester ascend through the skylight on to the roof: we heard him call "Bertha!" We saw him approach her; and then, ma'am, she yelled, and gave a spring, and the next minute she lay smashed on the pavement.'

It is clear from the form of words ('I witnessed and several more witnessed') that the innkeeper (formerly the Thornfield butler) is parroting verbatim his testimony at the coroner's inquest. As a pensioner of the Rochesters, he doubtless said what was required. There is no clear evidence that Edward went up to the burning roof to save Bertha – it could well be that he said something, inaudible to those below, that drove her to jump. His 'Bertha!' may have been uttered in a threatening tone. At the very least Mr Rochester, if no wife-murderer, might be thought indictable for manslaughter by virtue of persistent neglect. There have been previous warnings that Bertha is a threat to herself, and to others, under the gin-sodden care of Mrs Poole. Who is responsible for the fire at Thornfield – the madwoman, the drunk woman, or the husband who, despite these warnings, did not dismiss the drunk woman and put the madwoman under proper supervision? Is Edward Rochester a man to whom we entrust Jane Eyre with confidence, should she suffer a *crise de nerfs* later in life?

The main grounds for a reversal of the traditional antipathy towards Bluebeard the wife-killer are stated by Rochester himself in his explanations to Jane after their disastrously interrupted wedding. Edward was spoiled as a child. It is only late in life that he has gained moral maturity. His father and elder brother intended he should marry money, and conspired with the Mason family in Jamaica to unite him with Bertha. He was kept in the dark as to the madness rampant in the Mason line. Besotted by lust he married, only to discover that his much older wife was incorrigibly 'intemperate and unchaste' (less unchaste, perhaps, than Edward Rochester during his ten-years' philandering through the ranks of 'English ladies, French comtesses, Italian signoras, and German Gräfinnen'). But before the aggrieved husband can use her vile adulteries as grounds for divorce, Bertha cheats him by falling victim to the Mason curse. Lunatics cannot be held responsible in law for their acts. Edward is chained to Bertha. He brings her to England, where no one knows he is married. Nor shall they know. Servants who are necessarily aware of her existence assume she is 'my bastard half-sister; my cast-off mistress'. He is free to range Europe in search of sexual relief from mistresses not yet cast off. Sexual fulfilment eludes him. Only another marriage will answer his needs. Bigamy it must be.

Is Bluebeard-Rochester justified in his attempted act of bigamy? Are there mitigating circumstances, or just a middle-aged roué's glib excuses? In answering the question it is necessary first to determine the date of the action: more particularly, whether Rochester's foiled union with Jane takes place before or after the English Marriage Act of 1835. It was this act which clearly stated that marriage with a mad spouse could not be dissolved if the spouse were sufficiently sane at the time of the ceremony to understand the nature of the contract involved. Subsequent lunacy was no grounds for divorce even if compounded with other offences (violence, infidelity, desertion, cruelty). If the marriage in *Jane Eyre* is construed as taking place after 1835, then Edward is clearly guilty of a serious felony (intent to commit bigamy). It would be the responsibility of the clergyman, Mr Wood, to report Rochester (and Mr Carter, the physician, who criminally conspired with him) to the police. It is one of the small mysteries in *Jane Eyre* that Rochester seems to suffer no consequences, nor any visits from the authorities, following the 'bigamous' service.

If the marriage ceremony is construed as taking place before the firmer legislation of 1835, then Rochester may have a case for thinking that his earlier marriage is either null, or dissoluble on grounds of Bertha's premarital deceits, her subsequent adulteries, or the fact that the marriage may not have been consummated. He persistently refers to his wife as 'Bertha Mason', not 'Bertha Rochester', which suggests that he does not regard himself as married to the horrible woman. A good lawyer might fudge the issue for his client – not sufficiently to get him off the hook, but sufficiently to suggest that he honestly felt himself justified in making a second marriage.

When, then, is *Jane Eyre* set? The 1944 Orson Welles film explicitly declares that the central events occur in 1839. But in the novel dates are a minefield. The Penguin Classics edition's editor, Michael Mason, has looked into them most clearly. He identifies two conflicting pieces of dating evidence. When she came over from France (a few months before Jane's arrival at Thornfield), Adèle recalls 'a great ship with a chimney that smoked – how it did smoke!' Steam-driven vessels were plying up and down the eastern coast of Britain as early as 1821. Scott travelled down by one ('the Edinburgh') to the Coronation in 1821. Like Adèle, he found the vessel exceptionally smoky and he nicknamed it the 'New Reekie'. Cross-channel steam services seem to have started later in the 1820s.

If steam-driven ships are momentarily glimpsed (or smelled) in *Jane Eyre*, steam-engined trains are wholly absent. This is the prelapsarian world of the stage-coach. When Jane waits for her coach at the George Inn at Millcote she has leisure to examine the furniture. On the wall there are a number of prints: 'including a portrait of George the Third, and another of the Prince of Wales, and a representation of the death of Wolfe'. Clearly this is some point before the mid-1830s, when Millcote (Leeds) would have been served by the railway. But it would be interesting to know how faded those prints on the wall are. George III died in 1820; his son ceased to be Prince of Wales, and became Prince Regent, in 1811. West's famous picture of the death of Wolfe as engraved by John Boydell was most popular from around 1790 to 1810.

The clearest but most perplexing date-marker occurs late in the narrative, when Jane is with St John Rivers at Morton School. On 5 November (an anti-Papist holiday) St John brings Jane 'a book for evening solace'. It is 'a poem: one of those genuine productions so often vouchsafed to the fortunate public of those days – the golden age of modern literature. Alas! the readers of our era are less favoured . . . while I was eagerly glancing at the bright pages of *Marmion* (for *Marmion* it was), St John stooped to examine my drawing.'

Scott's long narrative poem *Marmion* was published in late February 1808 as a luxurious quarto, costing a guinea and a half. The month doesn't fit, although the year might be thought to chime with the earlier 'Prince of Wales' reference. But 1808 makes nonsense of critical elements in the characters' prehistories. It would give Jane, for instance, a birth-date of 1777. It would mean that Rochester impregnated Céline with Adèle (if he is indeed the little girl's father) around 1799. We would have to picture him, an Englishman, gallivanting round France during the Napoleonic Wars, crossing paths with the Scarlet Pimpernel and Sidney Carton. Those wars would still be going on in the background of the main action of *Jane Eyre*.

Seagoing steamers aside, Charlotte Brontë's novel does not 'feel' as if it is taking place in the first decade of the nineteenth century. There are numerous incidental allusions which place it at least a couple of decades later.[2] What seems most likely is that the 'new publication' of *Marmion* is the 'Magnum Opus' edition of 1834. This cheap edition (which came out with Scott's collected works) was hugely popular, and cost six shillings – more appropriate to the frugal pocket of St John Rivers than the de luxe version of 1808. It is quite possible that what Brontë is recalling in this little digression is the excitement which the purchase of the same, Magnum Opus, volume excited at Haworth Parsonage when she was nineteen.

A 'best date' for the main action of *Jane Eyre* would be the early to mid-1830s – a year or two before the critical date of 1835, which may be seen as foreshadowing but not as yet clearly defining the grounds for divorce or annulment. This historical setting would not exonerate Rochester's intended bigamy, but in the legally blurred context of pre-1835 it would not be as deliberately felonious an act as it would be in the film's 1839.

Rochester is an inscrutable man whom we never know on the inside. If we want to prognosticate whether, in the years of their marriage, he will make Jane Eyre happy, it is important to extricate his motives for marrying her in the first place – more particularly the series of events that lead to his dropping Blanche Ingram in favour of 'You – poor and obscure, and small and plain as you are'.

When Mr Rochester brings Blanche Ingram and her grand entourage to Thornfield Hall, there is every expectation of an imminent happy event. 'I saw he was going to marry her,' says Jane and so, apparently, does everyone else. Negotiations have been in train for some time. Lawyers have been consulting. It is common knowledge that the Ingram estate is entailed, which is why they are smiling on a match with an untitled suitor who happens to be very wealthy. It augurs well that Blanche has the physical attributes to which Rochester is addicted. Like her predecessor, Miss Ingram is 'moulded like a Dian'; she has the same 'strapping' beauty and jet-black tresses that captivated Edward in Jamaica fifteen years before.

The visit of the Ingram party calls for unprecedented preparations at the Hall, as Jane observes:

> I had thought all the rooms at Thornfield beautifully clean and well-arranged: but it appears I was mistaken. Three women were got to help; and such scrubbing, such brushing, such washing of paint and beating of carpets, such taking down and putting up of pictures, such polishing of mirrors and lustres, such lighting of fires in bed-rooms, such airing of sheets and feather-beds on hearths, I never beheld, either before or since.

The prenuptial junketing at Thornfield is interrupted by the unannounced arrival of Richard Mason from the West Indies. Rochester is not present to greet him (he is mounting his gypsy fortune-teller charade), but his reaction on being told of the Banquo visitation at his feast is dramatic:

> 'A stranger! – no: who can it be? I expected no one: is he gone?'
> 'No: he said he had known you long, and that he could take the liberty of installing himself till you returned.'
> 'The devil he did! Did he give his name?'
> 'His name is Mason, sir; and he comes from the West Indies: from Spanish Town, in Jamaica, I think.'
> Mr Rochester was standing near me: he had taken my hand, as if to lead me to a chair. As I spoke, he gave my wrist a convulsive grip; the smile on his lips froze: apparently a spasm caught his breath.
> 'Mason! – the West Indies!' he said, in the tone one might fancy a speaking automaton to enounce its single words.

There follows Mason's disastrous interview with his demented sister, uproar in the house, and a new bond of intimacy between Rochester and Jane. Shortly after Mason has gone (back to Jamaica, as Rochester thinks), Jane is called to the Reeds' house fifty miles away at Gateshead. There she remains a month, settling old scores. After her return, Mr Rochester is then himself away for some weeks. During this interval 'nothing was said of the master's marriage, and I saw no preparation going on for such an event'. It seems from a later conversation with Jane that Rochester has suddenly decided to put Miss Ingram to the test, and found her wanting in affection. 'I caused a rumour to reach her that my fortune was not a third of what was supposed, and after that I represented myself to see the result: it was coldness both from her and her mother.'

Having found Blanche and her mother lacking in warmth towards him, Edward proposes to Jane. It is no fashionable wedding that he offers. Their union will be private, furtive even. There are no relatives (apart from the distant Mrs Fairfax) on his side, and as Jane puts it (with an allusion to the dragonish Lady Ingram), 'There will be no-one to meddle, sir. I have no kindred to interfere.' There is a month of courtship – long enough for the banns to be discreetly called. Three short months after the world supposed Edward Rochester to be affianced to Miss Ingram, Rochester takes Jane Eyre up the aisle. The difference between the two planned weddings could not be greater. After the ceremony with Jane, the newly-weds will leave immediately for London. There is to be no wedding breakfast. The ceremony itself takes place in a deserted church. There are 'no groomsmen, no bridesmaids, no relatives' present. The assembled congregation is one person – Mrs Fairfax (what Rochester is to do for witnesses is not clear). The proceedings are then interrupted by the two strangers whom Jane has seen lurking around the graveyard: 'Mr Rochester has a wife now living,' it is proclaimed. The strangers are, of course, Rochester's bad-penny brother-in-law and a London solicitor.

This is the second time that Richard Mason has arrived to foil Rochester's imminent marriage. On both occasions his appearance is out of the blue and uncannily timely. At Thornfield

Hall, Rochester evidently thinks his brother-in-law dead, gone mad like the rest of the Masons, or safely ignorant of what is going on 3,000 miles away. Why does Richard turn up at this critical moment in Rochester's life, and what does he say to his brother-in-law about the law that joins them, and the impending 'marriage' with the Hon. Miss Ingram? After seeing him off Rochester clearly thinks that Richard is on his way back to Jamaica. He refers twice to this fact. But Richard Mason, it emerges in the Thornfield church, is not safely in the West Indies. Moreover, during the three intervening months he has had sent him a copy of Edward and Bertha Rochester's marriage certificate.

Who informed Mason of details of the forthcoming nuptials with Jane Eyre? It would have to be some insider in possession of two privileged pieces of knowledge: (1) the date, exact time, and place of the clandestine marriage – something known only to the two principals, the clergyman, and the three servants at Thornfield Hall; (2) that Richard Mason was the brother-in-law of Rochester's still-living wife, Bertha.

As Rochester later discloses, only four people in England are in possession of that second piece of information: himself, Bertha during her lucid periods, Carter the physician, and Grace Poole. There is, however, one other who may have penetrated the mystery. Rochester suspects that his distant kinswoman Mrs Fairfax 'may . . . have suspected something'. Certain of her remarks suggest that this is very likely. Mrs Fairfax, alone of all the Thornfield household, dismisses out of hand the likelihood that her relative will ever marry Blanche Ingram ('I should scarcely fancy Mr Rochester would entertain an idea of the sort'). And Mrs Fairfax is very alarmed when she subsequently learns that Jane is to marry her master, and very urgent in her dissuasions. It is also relevant that, immediately after the wedding débâcle, Rochester dismisses Mrs Fairfax from his employment at Thornfield. Nor is she called back after his blinding, when her presence, as his only living relative and former housekeeper, would seem desirable.

The most likely construction to put on this series of events is the following. Rochester had every intention of marrying Blanche Ingram, until the unexpected arrival of Richard Mason at Thornfield Hall. Who summoned him? Mrs Fairfax (although Rochester probably thought at the time that it was an unlucky coincidence). We do not know what was said between the two men. But Richard, timid though he is, would hardly give his blessing to bigamy, and the threat of exposure would be implied, if not uttered. His hopes with Blanche dashed, Rochester still longed for a wife. Another marriage in high life, such as the Rochester–Ingram affair, would attract huge publicity. That option was now too dangerous. Having packed Richard Mason back to the other side of the globe, Rochester put his mind to a partner whom he might marry without anyone knowing. He wanted nothing to get into newspapers which might subsequently find their way to the West Indies. Up to this point, Rochester must have thought of Jane Eyre as a potential future mistress. Now, with Blanche Ingram out of play, she was to be promoted. Carter was somehow squared. Poole was no problem; neither was Bertha. But, unfortunately for Rochester, Jane wrote to her uncle in Madeira, who fortuitously conveyed the news to Richard

Mason (who happened to be in Madeira for his health). We can assume that it was Mrs Fairfax, again, who alerted Mason as to the exact time and place of the wedding (something that Jane did not know, when she wrote). He in turn took legal advice and came back to Thornfield with his legally drawn-up 'impediment'. At this point, his marriage hopes in ruins, Rochester discerned who had betrayed him and sent Mrs Fairfax 'away to her friends at a distance'. Being the man he is, he also settled an annuity on her, presumably with the understanding that she stay out of his presence for ever (she is not mentioned in Jane's ten-years-after epilogue).

Bluntly, Rochester proposed to Jane as a *faute de mieux* – the *mieux* being Blanche Ingram. The notion sometimes advanced that the Ingram courtship was a charade designed to 'test' Jane is unconvincing. There was no need to test her, and if there were a need something much less elaborate might be devised (at the very least, something that might not land Rochester in a breach-of-promise suit). With many of Rochester's amoral acts (his adoption of Adèle, for example) there is a kind of careless grandeur. His courtship of Jane Eyre, by contrast, has something sneaking about it. Would he have proposed to the governess had Mason not arrived to foil his courtship of the society beauty? Probably not.

Like Samson, Rochester is ultimately humbled by tribulation and physical mutilation. 'A sightless block', he discovers Christianity and for the first time in his adult life has 'begun to pray'. But again, Jane would seem to be a *faute de mieux*. Supposing Edward Rochester had emerged from the blazing ruins of Thornfield with his limbs and organs intact, would it have been Jane he cried for at midnight? Possibly, possibly not. Blind and crippled, no comtesse, Blanche Ingram, or signorina will have him now. Only Jane will. Doubtless if, instead of killing Bluebeard, the wife's brothers had merely blinded him and cut off a hand (with the threat that if he did not behave himself they would come back and cut off some more), the old rogue might have become a tolerably good husband. But what if, like Edward Rochester, after ten years of marriage, his sight were to return and – barring the minor blemish of a missing hand (common enough, and even rather glamorous in these post-war years) – Bluebeard still cut a handsome figure? Could one be entirely confident that his wife-killing ways would not return?

How Many Pianos Has Amelia Sedley?

Like other well-brought-up girls of her era and class (early nineteenth century, London *nouveau riche)*, Amelia Sedley has
been taught to sing and play the piano. She is neither as gifted
in this department nor as industrious as her bosom friend at
Miss Pinkerton's Academy, Becky Sharp. Miss Sharp, we are
told, 'was already a musician' when she was taken in as a non-
paying boarder, and she practises 'incessantly'. None the less,
Amelia can handle the instrument well enough to make a private recital the pretext of flirting with George Osborne in the
'back drawing-room'. It is there that the Sedleys' family piano
is situated ('as pianos usually are', the narrator notes – pianos,
incidentally, are omnipresent in *Vanity Fair*). This back-
drawing-room piano makes a later appearance at the auction
where Mr Hammerdown disposes of the ruined Mr Sedley's
household effects two years later. It is, we are informed as it
comes up for sale, a 'state grand piano'. Presumably it is as
vulgar a piece of furniture as the 'great carved-legged, leather-
cased grand piano' in the Osbornes' hateful upstairs drawing-
room, in their house on the other side of Russell Square.

At the auction, the point is made that there are in fact two
pianos in the Sedleys' household. Amelia has, as her private
possession in her own room, 'a little square piano'. It is with
the changing fortunes of this modest instrument over the years
that I am concerned here. It first makes an appearance in
Chapter 2. Amelia has brought Becky back to stay with her for
a week or so at Russell Square, before Miss Sharp takes up her
new position as governess at Queen's Crawley. Becky has
clearly never been to the Sedleys' home before. As soon as they
arrive, Amelia excitedly shows Rebecca 'over every room of

the house, and everything in every one of her drawers; and her books, and her piano, and her dresses, and all her necklaces, brooches, laces, and gimcracks'. Guessing from the context, 'her piano' is the little square instrument in her bedroom, not the great monster downstairs.

The little square piano is not heard of again until months later, in Chapter 17 ('How Captain Dobbin Bought a Piano'), where it briefly has a starring role. It is the auction following Sedley's bankruptcy and Dobbin, good-hearted as ever, has resolved to buy the little piano and return it to Amelia. But his agent finds that someone else is interested. To the auctioneer's surprise the bids rise to twenty-five guineas, at which inflated level Dobbin secures the instrument. It emerges that his rival in the bidding has been Becky. She takes her loss with typical good spirits: 'I wish we could have afforded some of the plate,' she tells her husband, Rawdon (they are newly wed, and setting up house); 'Five-and-twenty guineas was monstrously dear for that little piano. We chose it at Broadwood's for Amelia, when she came from school. It only cost five-and-thirty then.' As the Oxford World's Classics note records: 'John Broadwood, the piano-maker, had his business in Great Pulteney Street. In 1782 he patented his hugely successful design for a domestic pianoforte.' There is already a small narrative inconsistency, however. Becky's recollection that the instrument was bought 'when Amelia came from school' indicates that it was acquired during that June 1813 holiday she spent at Russell Square, after the girls had left Miss Pinkerton's for good. But, in Chapter 2, it is suggested that Amelia already has a piano in her room. Are we to assume that the Broadwood is a replacement? Or, as seems more probable, is Becky fibbing?

Dobbin, having secured the piano, makes arrangements for it to be sent to the 'little house where the Sedley family had found refuge' after the crash. Tactfully, he does not accompany it with a note drawing attention to his generosity. A

desperate Amelia, clutching at straws, assumes that the piano
has come from George. Although their parents have called off
the engagement he still loves her, she deludes herself. At the
end of her note to George accompanying the return of his
presents ('made in happier days'), she adds a postscript: 'I shall
often play upon the piano – your piano. It was like you to send
it.' In their quarters at the barracks, George shows Dobbin
this letter, and he reads all of it. Surprisingly, there is no
recorded conversation along the lines of: 'Who the deuce sent
her that piano? You did, Dobbin? Gad! What a trump you are.'

The next day, Dobbin calls on the Sedleys in their refuge.
He finds Mrs Sedley 'greatly agitated by the arrival of the
piano, which, as she conjectured, *must* have come from
George, and was a signal of amity on his part'. Captain Dobbin, we are told, 'did not correct this error of the worthy lady'.
And he sets in motion the events that will lead to the marriage
of George and Amelia in defiance of old Osborne's tyrannic
prohibition and his (Dobbin's) own forlorn hope that Amelia
might one day be his.

At this point, we may digress to indicate where Thackeray
got the idea for this Broadwood square-piano sub-plot. In Volume II, Chapter 8 of *Emma*, the heroine learns from her
friend Mrs Cole that Jane Fairfax, who is staying with her aunt,
Miss Bates, has had a mysterious gift:

> Mrs Cole . . . had been calling on Miss Bates, and as soon as she
> entered the room had been struck by the sight of a pianoforté –
> a very elegant-looking instrument – not a grand, but a large-sized
> square pianoforté . . . this pianoforté had arrived from Broad-
> wood's the day before, to the great astonishment of both aunt
> and niece – entirely unexpected; that at first, by Miss Bates's ac-
> count, Jane herself was quite at a loss, quite bewildered to think
> who could possibly have ordered it – but now, they were both
> perfectly satisfied that it could be from only one quarter; – of
> course it must be from Col. Campbell.

No, as we later discover, it was not from the colonel, but from Jane's secret admirer, Frank Churchill. Frank, like Dobbin, does not enlighten the world, noting only with an enigmatic smile to Emma (who entirely misinterprets its meaning), 'It is a handsome present.' Thackeray evidently thought that this was too good a sub-plot to be used only once in English fiction.

After its return to the Sedley household the little square piano is lost once more in the background of *Vanity Fair*. It is glimpsed again when, shortly after her wedding, Amelia makes a trip to her parents, now in a cottage at Fulham (supported by an annuity from their nabob son, Jos). Things are going badly for Mrs Amelia Osborne. George is already kicking over the traces – spending too much, drinking too much, gambling too much and, as Amelia dare not admit to herself, consorting adulterously with other women. She falls down by the maidenly white bed she slept on as a girl and prays (prayers which, the narrator sternly informs us, we have no right to overhear). Then she goes downstairs and, to cheer up her father, 'She sat down at the piano which Dobbin had bought for her, and sang over all her father's favourite old songs.'

For twelve long years the little square piano disappears from view while momentous things happen. Napoleon is defeated, George is killed, Becky is presented to her sovereign then taken in adultery, Amelia loses Georgy to the Osbornes, everyone (including the piano) gets suddenly middle-aged. When a grizzled Major Dobbin, CB, returns in 1827 from India he makes his first call on the Sedleys, now in lodgings at Brompton. At last, he fondly hopes, he may make his proposals to Amelia. He is admitted into the Sedleys' drawing-room: 'whereof he remembered every single article of furniture, from the old brass ornamented piano, once a natty little instrument, Stothard maker, to the screens and the alabaster miniature tombstone, in the midst of which ticked Mr Sedley's gold watch'.

At the auction Becky specifically recalls the instrument's being bought at Broadwood's. Robert Stothard was Broadwood's great rival. They did not sell each other's pianos. There is more confusion to come. Dobbin is with Amelia a few days later, as arrangements are being made to move her family into Jos's grand new house (he has returned from India with Dobbin). To the major's pleasure, he sees that she has brought with her the piano:

> that little old piano which had now passed into a plaintive jingling old age, but which she loved for reasons of her own. She was a child when first she played on it: and her parents gave it her. It had been given to her again since, as the reader may remember, when her father's house was gone to ruin, and the instrument was recovered out of the wreck.

Dobbin's hopes are raised by Amelia's special attention to 'this old music-box'. He is glad she has kept it, he tells her:

> 'I was afraid you didn't care about it.'
> 'I value it more than anything I have in the world,' said Amelia.
> '*Do* you, Amelia?' cried the Major. The fact was, as he had bought it himself, though he never said anything about it, it never entered into his head to suppose that Emmy should think anybody else was the purchaser, and as a matter of course, he fancied that she knew the gift came from him. 'Do you, Amelia?' he said; and the question, the great question of all, was trembling on his lips, when Emmy replied –
> 'Can I do otherwise? – did not *he* give it me?'
> 'I did not know,' said poor old Dob, and his countenance fell.

The Indian fevers he has suffered from must have affected the major's brain. He was shown Amelia's letter to George in April 1815 mistakenly thanking him (George) for the gift of the piano. Shortly afterwards he (Dobbin) gallantly declined to correct Mrs Sedley's misapprehension that George was the donor. At that point in the narrative Dobbin clearly did know that Amelia mistakenly thought that the piano came from George, not him. There are other little mysteries swirling about the episode. Did Amelia and George never talk about the piano? Are we to assume he lied on the subject after their marriage, or deliberately left her in the dark? If so, it adds a new and uncharacteristically sly dimension to his villainy.

Shortly after the above exchange at Brompton, a mortified Amelia suddenly realises the truth: 'it was William who was the giver of the piano.' She now hates the thing: 'It was not George's relic. It was valueless now. The next time that old Sedley asked her to play, she said it was shockingly out of tune, that she had a headache, that she couldn't play.' The instrument is never heard of again in *Vanity Fair*. Perhaps Amelia keeps it, more likely it is thrown into some lumber-room and forgotten.

There are three problems in charting the long career of the little square piano. Did Amelia get it as a little girl, or did she buy it in company with Becky, as a young woman? Is it a Broadwood or a Stothard? Does Dobbin know that Amelia doesn't know who gave it to her? By tying oneself in knots, one can find ingenious solutions. There were more than one (perhaps as many as three) little pianos over the years at Russell Square – in his palmy days, old Sedley was certainly rich and doting enough to shower his daughter with expensive luxuries. Dobbin has hoped so obsessively that Amelia will love him that his memory has warped. Freudian analysis throws up any number of examples of this 'willed amnesia' phenomenon. When she made her remark about 'We chose it at Broadwood's . . . it only cost five-and-thirty,' Becky is not remembering an event, but prodding Rawdon to take her, that very minute, to the nearby emporium in Great Pulteney Street to buy her an instrument just like the one she has lost to Dobbin at auction.

Attractive as ingenuity is, it would be misplaced here. As Stephen Blackpool would say, 'it's aw a muddle' – but only if we read *Vanity Fair* the wrong way. What we learn from following the story of the piano is something important about Thackeray's writing habits, something to which we must adjust our own reading habits when we come to his novels. He loved long perspectives and the resonant recurrent detail. No author handles such effects better. But Thackeray could not be troubled, or was too hurried, to turn back the pages of his novel to see what he had written earlier. His memory – wonderfully sure in essentials – played tricks with small details, tricks that the reader happily indulges.

Whose Daughter Is Nancy?

The Good Soldier is, Eugene Goodheart claims, 'one of the most puzzling works of modern fiction'.[1] It is notoriously hard to make sense of Ford's characters, their backgrounds, and their actions. There is critical dissension on such issues as whether the title (in so far as it refers to Captain Edward Ashburnham's 'goodness') is ironic or not. The narrative is speckled with what look like factual contradictions (about such crucial data as when and where the Dowells first met the Ashburnhams). Close inspection reveals that the chronology is awry at almost every point. 'Is this', Martin Stannard asks, 'Fordian irony or simply carelessness about details?'[2] Should we lay the inconsistencies at the door of an artfully unreliable narrator (John Dowell), or at the door of a slipshod writer (Ford Madox Ford)? Some critics, Vincent Cheng for instance (who has assembled a convincing chronology of *The Good Soldier*), believe that Ford is writing in 'the French mode of *vraisemblance*', and that it is legitimate to ask 'what actually happens?'[3] with a reasonable expectation of getting 'right' answers. Other commentators, such as Frank Kermode, see *The Good Soldier* as the *locus classicus* of modernist indeterminacy. 'We are in a world of which it needs to be said not that plural readings are possible (for this is true of all narrative) but that the *illusion of the single right reading is possible no longer.*'[4]

I want to look at a puzzle highlighted by Ian Hamilton, reviewing the latest biography of Ford Madox Ford, by Max Saunders, in the *London Review of Books* (20 June 1996). A number of reviewers felt that the fifty-three pages of close exegesis which Saunders lavished on *The Good Soldier* might be too much of a good thing. Hamilton did not. He was particularly grateful for 'a single right reading' that Saunders brought to a traditionally difficult text:

> Saunders has found a real-life model for John Dowell and argues persuasively (with biographical support) that Ashburnham's suicide was forced on him by the knowledge that Nancy was actually his daughter. Has this theory been proposed before? Not that I know of. All in all, Saunders's *Good Soldier* chapter had the effect of altering my reading of a book I thought I knew – a book I thought was marred by Ashburnham's implausible exit. So I for one am grateful.

The Good Soldier is a text well trodden by critical explication and a couple of weeks later Edward Mendelson wrote to the *LRB* (18 July) pointing out that Dewy Ganzel had contributed a 'persuasive' article to the *Journal of Modern Literature* (July 1984), arguing that Nancy was Edward's natural daughter. The insight was not quite as new as Hamilton thought.

Questions of priority aside, what is the case for thinking that Edward's relationship with Nancy Rufford is not merely treacherous and adulterous, but incestuous? Prima facie it is odd that Edward reacts as remorsefully as he does to this last of his affairs. He is inhibited, as he tells Dowell, by a 'tabu' round Nancy. There are very few taboos in modern life; sleeping with one's daughter is certainly one of them. In other of his philanderings Ashburnham is wholly uninhibited. As far as we can make out he is a sexual addict, incapable of keeping his hands off any woman who takes his fancy. Prudence counts for nothing when his carnal pleasures are involved. He compromises his position in English society by assaulting a servant ('the Kilsyte girl') in a third-class railway carriage. In India, he seduces brother-officers' wives ('Mrs Major Basil', 'little Maisie Maidan'), exposing himself to blackmail and possible court-martial. He is prepared to bankrupt his estate and

publicly humiliate his wife by buying the favours of a cour-
tesan (La Dolciquita) for an outrageous £60,000. For nine
years he callously cuckolds his best friend, the gullible Dowell
(Florence meanwhile denies Dowell his conjugal rights on the
grounds of 'heart'). Florence, as Dowell belatedly discovers,
poisons herself when she believes Ashburnham has thrown her
over in favour of the much younger Nancy.

Why then should a late-life fling with Nancy precipitate
Edward's own suicide, Nancy's madness, and a nervous
breakdown in Leonora? The Ashburnhams, at least, must be
habituated to his incorrigible infidelity by now and it would
seem that the worst (Florence's death, financial ruin, a court-
case, blackmail) has already happened. It is true that Nancy is
Leonora's ward, but on past record this would prove no bar to
Edward's making her his mistress.

In explaining the traumatic effects of the Ashburnham–
Nancy affair, Ganzel points to some odd inconsistencies in the
accounts we are given of Nancy's background. First we are
told that Nancy was 'Leonora's only friend's only child', and
that 'she had lived with the Ashburnhams ever since she had
been of the age of thirteen, when her mother was said to have
committed suicide owing to the brutalities of her father'. Later
we are told that Nancy was sent to boarding-school and 'her
mother disappeared from her life at that time. A fortnight later
Leonora came to the convent and told her that her mother
was dead.' Finally, nine years later, we learn that 'Nancy Rufford had a letter from her mother. It came whilst Leonora was
talking to Edward, or Leonora would have intercepted it as
she had intercepted others. It was an amazing and horrible
letter.' What amazing horrors the letter contains we are not
specifically told – except that she may not be Colonel Rufford's
daughter (he has retired from the army, and is now a tea-
planter in Ceylon).

There are further mysteries about Mrs Rufford: it is implied
at one point that she has descended to the condition of a com-

mon street-walker in Glasgow. Then it emerges that she is living reasonably prosperously, with a man whose telephone number Ashburnham knows well. There are, as Ganzel points out, loose ends here, and the explanation he comes to is 'that Nancy is Edward Ashburnham's natural daughter'. Edward knew, Leonora knew, and after receiving the 'horrible' letter from her mother, Nancy knew. The only person who doesn't know is the narrator, Dowell (and the bulk of his readers, one might add). Just as he couldn't see what was going on under his nose with Florence and Ashburnham, Dowell is blind to the relationship between Edward and Nancy.

If, against Kermode's instruction, one believes in 'single right readings', this would seem to be extraordinarily satisfactory. Certainly Max Saunders found it so: 'I had known the novel for nine years', he writes (echoing the nine years the Dowells knew the Ashburnhams), 'before the thought occurred to me, but then immediately details began to fall into place.'[5] Saunders's 'thought' is framed slightly more cautiously than Ganzel puts it: 'The girl with whom Ashburnham has become infatuated might be his own illegitimate daughter.' 'Might' leaves open the possibility that Ashburnham and Leonora cannot be sure – it's a wise philanderer that knows his own daughter. But none the less the 'touch of incest' insight is, for Saunders, the key to *The Good Soldier*, discovered only after years wrestling with the text.

Attractive as it is, the 'Nancy is Edward's daughter' interpretation is flawed. There is, one may note, no physical resemblance. Edward is fair-haired ('golden-haired' as he grows older), with striking porcelain-blue eyes. Nancy has 'the heaviest head of black hair that I have ever come across'. Given recessive genes, hair colour is by no means a clinching factor. Dates are. When the four principals meet at Nauheim in summer 1904, Edward is thirty-three. This gives a birth-date of 1870 or 1871. When Florence kills herself it is 1913, and Nancy is something between twenty-one and twenty-two, which gives a birth-date of 1891 or 1892. When Nancy was conceived (1890 or 1891), Edward was between twenty and twenty-one. It was at the age of twenty-two that he married Leonora, at which time he was, Dowell tells us, 'almost as pure in mind as Leonora herself. It is odd how a boy can have his virgin intelligence untouched in this world.' Edward's career in extramarital 'libertinism' begins with the Kilsyte case, in 1895.

Dates are notoriously slippery in *The Good Soldier*. But those I have listed here are among the most reliable we can determine in the novel. They are the pegs on which the narrative hangs. If they are not reliable, nothing is – even the names of the characters and the places they visit. It is hard, almost inconceivable, to picture 'virginal' Edward in his early twenties fathering Nancy, by the wife of a Scottish officer in a Highland regiment. Such acts belong to his later life. Probably, like the mad (if she is mad) governess in James's *The Turn of the Screw*, Nancy's paternity will become one of modernism's chewed bones. But the balance of evidence is against its being Edward Ashburnham.

Why Is the Monster Yellow?

Simon Levene writes wittily in response to *Is Heathcliff a Murderer?*, correcting an error and pointing out an unobserved other puzzle in *Frankenstein*:

> without seeming ragingly pedantic, may I mention p. 27, where you refer to a 'metallic bolt' attaching [the monster's] head to its body? In fact, it is not a bolt but the ends of the electrodes through which the electricity flows into the monster. More to the point, why should Victor Frankenstein ever *construct* a body? Why wouldn't *one* body have done quite as well?

Mr Levene's 'one body' question sticks in the mind. After wrestling with it, I would offer two possible lines of explanation. The first is to be found in the epigraph from Milton's *Paradise Lost* (x. 743–5) on the novel's title-page:

> Did I request thee, Maker, from my clay
> To mould Me man? Did I solicit thee
> From darkness to promote me? –

As commentators have often noted, Mary Shelley's novel conforms closely to Milton's epic as source text. We are not shown how God creates Adam from his constituent clay. But it is quite clear how he creates that lesser order of creation, Eve. He takes a body part – Adam's rib – and out of that *membrum* makes woman. This notion of making the whole new person out of the part(s) of another person is clearly alluded to in Mary Shelley's description of the scientist–hero's midnight raids: 'I collected bones from charnel houses; and disturbed,

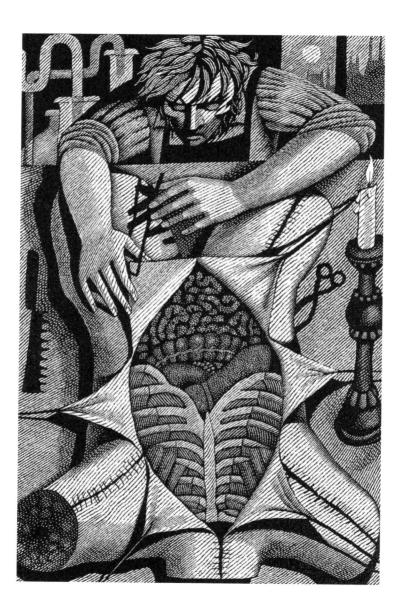

with profane fingers, the tremendous secrets of the human frame . . . The dissecting room and the slaughter-house furnished many of my materials.' Victor seems to be doing two things here: investigating the anatomy of the 'human frame' and assembling the wherewithal – the 'Adam's ribs' – with which to compose such a frame.

The other objection to Victor's using an intact body for his monster is theological. There are any number of accounts of hanged criminals being taken down too soon, and crossing back from death to life. Much fiction has built itself around the conceit. As Marilyn Butler notes in her Oxford World's Classics edition of the 1818 text:

> a number of well-known attempts had been made to induce life, whether by animating single-cell creatures, such as body parasites, or by reviving dead bodies, including executed criminals. Some of the best-known were associated with Luigi Galvani.

The problem (for Mary Shelley) was that such back-from-the-dead survivors – prisoners taken down prematurely from the gallows, for example – come back not as newborn babes, but as their former selves. So too, if Galvani had succeeded in reviving a dead body it would have returned as its former self. Shelley wanted 'creation', not 'resurrection'. It was necessary to dissolve the pre-existing personalities (and by implication the multiple 'souls') of the bodies from whom the miscellaneous parts were gathered.

Significantly, this is an area in which the archetypal film version, that by James Whale in 1931, goes directly against Mary Shelley's portrayal. The deformed servant, Fritz, is shown breaking into the anatomy laboratory to steal a brain, and – having accidentally dropped the brain of a genius – takes instead that of a psychopathic criminal (without telling his master). We are to assume that traces of the criminal's previous criminality infect the monster, although Whale does not follow up this line in the melodramatic middle and late sections of the film narrative.

It would be interesting to know how Mary Shelley imagined that a brain could be transplanted, without trailing clouds of the previous owner's character. She sidesteps the problem by artfully hazing over the description of how the monster is actually made. And she goes on to imply (without ever clearly asserting) that the monster is less a kind of physiological jigsaw man – assembled from bits and pieces gathered from hither and yon – than a culture *grown* from a soup, or distillate, extracted from all the *membra disjecta* Victor has assembled from his midnight raids. Wisely, perhaps, Mary Shelley does not go into detail about what goes on in Victor's 'filthy workshop' as, to their detriment, all film versions of *Frankenstein* have done.

Shelley does, however, go into some detail about the physical appearance of the newborn (newly assembled) monster:

> It was already one in the morning; the rain pattered dismally against the panes, and my candle was nearly burnt out, when, by the glimmer of the half-extinguished light, I saw the *dull yellow eye* of the creature open; it breathed hard, and a convulsive motion agitated its limbs.
>
> How can I describe my emotions at this catastrophe, or how delineate the wretch whom with such infinite pains and care I had endeavoured to form? His limbs were in proportion, and I had selected his features as beautiful. Beautiful! – Great God! His *yellow skin* scarcely covered the work of muscles and arteries beneath; his hair was of a lustrous black, and flowing; his teeth of a pearly whiteness; but these luxuriances only formed a more horrid contrast with his watery eyes, that seemed almost of the same colour as the *dun white sockets* in which they were set, his shrivelled complexion, and straight black lips. [My emphasis]

Jonathan Grossman raises an interesting query about this. 'Last semester' (i.e. winter 1997), he writes:

I heard Professor Anne Mellor (whose work I very much like) give an interesting talk about Frankenstein's monster as an 'Oriental' menace. The problem with the argument was that it rested wholly on the thinnest of evidence: the creature's infamous yellow eyes and yellow skin. It seems to me a long way from these yellow eyes and yellow skin to the 'Yellow Peril'. How does one build an Asian body out of the corpses of Europeans?

I tend to agree with Professor Grossman – thought-provoking as Professor Mellor's thesis is. But, as Grossman says, the yellow eyes are perplexing. He pursues the problem, arguing that we should not assume 'that the irises themselves are a cat-like yellow'. As he confesses, Victor has raided slaughterhouses in his midnight expeditions. But it is extremely unlikely (unless he ventured as far afield as Korea, which would give substance to the Yellow Peril hypothesis) that he found cats' heads in the local shambles or butcher-shop. We assume, therefore, that it is the 'whites' of the monster's eyes which are yellow – or 'dun white'.

Grossman concludes that 'the poor creature is born with jaundice.' He called up a doctor friend, who confirmed that 'the whites of the eyes as well as the skin do turn yellow and that it is one of the main signs of jaundice. Diagnosis: a liver condition? Bad liver transplant?'

There is a persuasive biographical explanation for the yellow monster being jaundiced. As commentators (particularly feminist commentators) have noted, the creation scene in *Frankenstein*, and the concomitant disgust of Victor for his creation, can be read as an allegory of post-natal shock and depression. In February 1815 Mary Wollstonecraft, aged seventeen, gave premature birth to a daughter – Clara – who died a few days later; of what, we do not know. In January 1816 she gave birth to a son, William. Mary and Percy Shelley did not marry until December 1816. While she was completing *Frankenstein* in May 1817 Mary was pregnant with her third

child. She knew about post-natal depression and was familiar
with the physical appearance of newborn children.

Jaundice is a very common and (to the mother's eye) alarming condition in newborn babies. One (or both) of Mary's
children may well, one assumes, have been born with it, possibly fatally in Clara's case. Interestingly, no later references
seem to be made to the monster's having a yellow skin or eyes.
He is 'ugly' and 'loathsome', but not – as far as we know –
'yellow'.

How Does Ruth End Up in Wales?

Frances Twinn, a graduate student working on the fiction of Elizabeth Gaskell, points to a troubling inconsistency at the heart of *Ruth*. The narrative opens with a depiction of the poor but genteel heroine apprenticed to a harsh milliner, Mrs Mason, in 'an assize town in one of the eastern counties'. It is 'many years ago'. We should picture, it seems, a sleepy county town like Ipswich or Norwich in the 1830s. The heroine, Ruth Hilton, is an orphan. Her mother had been the daughter of a Norfolk curate – a 'delicate, fine lady'; her father had been a farmer – a good-hearted but tragically unlucky man. The delicate Mrs Hilton died early of physical exhaustion, unable to cope with the physical demands of being a farmer's wife. He followed soon after of a broken heart and bankruptcy. Ruth, alone in the world, falls into the unfeeling custody of a 'hard-headed' guardian, who disposes of the waif to Mrs Mason so as to be rid of her, at the small expense of her indenture fee.

At the shire-hall New-Year celebrations, fifteen-year-old Ruth Hilton catches the eye of a twenty-three-year-old sprig of the gentry. In return for the girl's deftly mending the torn dress of his partner (the haughty Miss Duncombe), Henry Bellingham gives Ruth a camellia. The gentleman's trifling gift goes to the humble dressmaker's heart. Over the following six months Bellingham pursues Ruth. She is a beautiful girl – although chronically shy and deferential. It is not clear whether he intends to seduce her or to enjoy some risky flirtation: he is no villain, merely feckless. She is no trollop, merely innocent of the ways of the world. As Mrs Gaskell emphasises time and again, she has no *mother* to guide her.

On a nostalgic visit to her former home, Ruth is seen in the company of Bellingham by Mrs Mason and dismissed on the spot ('I'll have no slurs on the character of my apprentices ... I shall write and tell your guardian tomorrow.') Her guardian, of course, will now disown her – glad to be rid of the expense. Ruth is now that most unfortunate of Victorian women, a 'castaway'. Bellingham at first seems perplexed as to what to do: 'It is very unfortunate; for, you see, I did not like to name it to you before, but, I believe – I have business, in fact, which obliges me to go to town to-morrow – to London, I mean; and I don't know when I shall be able to return.'

The news that he too is about to abandon her plunges Ruth into paralytic despair. But, on the spur of the moment, Bellingham sees a solution: 'Ruth, would you go with me to London ... you must come with me, love, and trust to me.' It is the serpent's invitation. 'Young, and innocent, and motherless' – Ruth succumbs. Bellingham goes off to get the carriage that will carry the young milliner to her eternal shame.

Chapter 4 of Gaskell's novel (which has been rattling along) ends: 'Ruth was little accustomed to oppose the wishes of any one – obedient and docile by nature, and unsuspicious and innocent of any harmful consequences. She entered the carriage, and drove towards London.' As Mrs Twinn puts it:

> So the reader is left expecting the couple to arrive in London as they turn over the page. Therefore it is with some astonishment that the reader finds himself transported to 'a little mountain village in North Wales'. Why did Gaskell change her mind? Are there any clues that she has intended to do this all along?

It's a good question. Without explanation or any further mention of London, we find ourselves at the beginning of Chapter 5 in the Welsh village Mrs Twinn mentions. It is unnamed, but some seventeen miles from 'Pen trê Voelas' – somewhere in the north of the principality, near Snowdonia we may guess. It is early July – only two months can have passed since Chapter 4 (as Mrs Twinn calculates). It turns out that the inn in which Henry and Ruth are now staying is familiar to him from his varsity days. He knows 'its dirt of old', as Gaskell ominously puts it. He and his fellow undergraduates used to bring 'reading parties' there.

From the disreputable nature of Mrs Jenny Morgan, the landlady, it is clear that the inn does not uphold strict rules of morality among its patrons. 'Young men will be young men,' Mrs Morgan thinks indulgently when she apprehends that Ruth is 'not his wife . . . His wife would have brought her maid, and given herself twice as many airs about the sitting rooms.' Ruth, presumably, is wearing gloves, so the ring, or its absence, is invisible to the innkeeper's sharp eyes. Clearly 'Mrs Bellingham' – as she will have been introduced – has *some* luggage (at least a change of clothes and toilet articles) with her, if no maid. From Mrs Morgan's indulgent reflections, we may assume that when the young students last came, three years ago, they brought some loose company ('Cyprians') with them in addition to their books. Ruth is just such another *belle amie*.

It is said that the couple intend only 'a week's enjoyment of that Alpine scenery', although it seems from other comments that he may be looking for a house to set her up in. Even in private conversation Ruth still timidly addresses Bellingham as 'sir', but it is clear they have slept together and are currently sharing a bed. Although she does not yet know it, Ruth is already pregnant with baby Leonard. Bellingham, ominously, is beginning to be bored with the little dressmaker. It has been the best part of a week and the evenings drag without livelier company. But before their relationship can work itself to the inevitable conclusion, Bellingham falls into a fever and is repossessed by his vengeful mother, who self-righteously casts out the little minx who has clearly entrapped her son.

So begins Ruth's long travail as a Victorian lone parent and the main business of the novel. But the question remains, why does it begin in North Wales, not London? It may, of course, be a bad join in the narrative. But there is a possible explanation, more flattering to Gaskell's art and her tender sensibility. The first question that strikes the reader is: did Henry Bellingham *really* have to go to London? Probably not. His uncertain and stumbling choice of words ('I *believe* – I have business') and his claim to have just this moment remembered that he has business in the capital suggest a spur-of-the-moment brainwave. It strikes him that, since Ruth is fortuitously homeless and friendless, now is the time to make his move.

Secondly, what is the route that the couple have taken in Bellingham's carriage? If they are going from the general direction of an 'eastern assize town' to northern Wales, they would almost certainly have to go cross-country through London. So it would not be illogical for the carriage to drive, on its first leg, in that direction, as we are told at the end of Chapter 4. What subsequently happens in London? First, Bellingham would put up in some convenient (but discreet) hostelry and do what seducers do when innocent young things fall into their clutches. Then, on the next day, he would buy some clothes and other necessaries for his new mistress (who has left without luggage – not that her milliner's-apprentice outfits would be appropriate for her new station in life as 'Mrs Bellingham').

It would be difficult for Bellingham to stay in town – his mother might find out. She might tell Ruth's guardian. The girl is fifteen – three years over the age of consent for sexual intercourse but six years below the age of consent for marriage in England. It would look bad if Ruth laid a bastard to his charge in the 'assize town' where he lived, and claimed that he had promised marriage. Even if this disaster were averted, Mrs Mason might find out what has happened to one of her charges (she is *in loco parentis*) and make all sorts of trouble. Where would be a convenient place to install the young lady where she might be available, but not publicly visible? As a twenty-three-year-old, Henry has little experience in such worldly matters as setting up a mistress. But, he remembers, there was that place in Wales where, as a student, he and his friends had that jolly time, and where the landlady was so accommodating. Just the ticket! The journey is around two hundred miles, and they will arrive in a couple of days in his hired carriage. He will find some remote (and cheaply rented) house for Ruth well out of the world's eye. He can visit her at his discretion. The name 'Bellingham' will mean nothing in rural Wales.

Why did Gaskell not describe the London episode: the defloration of Ruth? Because it was painful and (as with the murder in *Mary Barton*) she did not like painful scenes and would go to some lengths to avoid them. Secondly, it would have been difficult to present Ruth to the reader in such a way as not to make her seem in some part guilty of her own downfall – unless, that is, she also presented Bellingham as a Lovelace-like rapist (something else she did not want to do). Ruth did not have to get in the carriage and go to London. She could have taken her chances with her guardian, explained her innocence to Mrs Mason, even have gone to the local clergyman. Even in the London inn – or house of assignation – where her pearl without price was lost, Ruth did not *have to* give in (assuming that Henry did not force her). A firm 'no' would have sufficed to preserve her virtue. A decent veil is drawn, so that we do not think too ill of the poor motherless child. The ever-motherly Mrs Gaskell will not cast the first stone.[1]

What Kills Lady Dedlock?

A disagreement between two Dickensian critics highlights a central puzzle in *Bleak House*. In a 1983 article, entitled 'The Fever of *Bleak House*', Fred Schwarzbach noted that 'disease plays a central part' in the novel's plot, 'as both subject and metaphor'.[1] Few readers will disagree. Many characters in *Bleak House* die, of many ailments, ranging from opium poisoning, through cerebral stroke, to that most controversial of causes of death, 'spontaneous combustion'. But 'What is not clear, and has puzzled modern critics', Schwarzbach notes, 'is why Dickens has Jo contract smallpox. Should he not have written instead about cholera, the most feared of all fevers in mid-Victorian England, which recently had ravaged the nation in the epidemic of 1848–9?'

Two suggested explanations are offered, both pertinent to the novel's design. Smallpox (unlike typhus) is contagious and serves a 'symbolic' function by linking all the otherwise divergent lines of character and action. 'Connection' is a major theme in the novel, and nothing connects like the pox. Secondly, on the level of plot device, the disease serves the practical purpose of 'disfiguring Esther so that no one will notice her resemblance to her mother'.

In a subsequent article, ' "Deadly Stains": Lady Dedlock's Death', Schwarzbach elaborates this insight, arguing that – although Dickens does not clearly indicate the fact – it *must* be smallpox that kills Lady Dedlock.[2] The moment of contagion occurs in Chapter 16 when, disguised in her servant's clothes, she pays a night-time visit to her lover, Captain Hawdon, resting in his pauper's 'berryin' place'. Dickens accompanies the contagious episode with a charnel-house description of the miasmic infection swirling around the graveyard, and its deadly deposits of 'witch ointment' and 'Tom's [i.e. Tom-all-alone's] slime'. In this gothic effusion, Schwarzbach detects a 'key detail' which 'evidently has escaped the notice of modern critics' in the sentence: 'The servant [i.e. Lady Dedlock in her maid's gown] shrinks into a corner – into a corner of that hideous archway, *with its deadly stains contaminating her dress*; and . . . so remains for some moments.' The stains are 'deadly' because they contain the virus (literally 'poison'). Dickens selected the scene for illustration in the serial version of the novel.

Smallpox, as Schwarzbach notes, has 'a variable incubation period', and it is the fever phase of this disease which, we are to assume, eventually kills Lady Dedlock. In her last hours, we are told by eyewitnesses that she is 'hoarse', 'pale', and 'unable to eat'; symptoms compatible with those of the smallpox fever (a sceptic might note, however, that they are symptomatic of much milder ailments than smallpox). Schwarzbach informs us that Victorians believed smallpox could lie dormant until 'a period when the physical system was fatigued or under stress – that is why Jo becomes seriously ill only after Bucket forces him to "move on" ceaselessly'.

Lady Dedlock is certainly under stress in the last two days of her life. Her world collapses with a letter accusing her of killing Tulkinghorn, and a visit from the obnoxious Guppy indicating that her secret past is secret no more. She will shortly be unmasked before the world as a 'harlot' (which she is) and charged as a murderess (which she is not). 'There is no escape but in death,' she resolves.

But she does not, in fact, kill herself – or at least not directly. It is morning. Dashing off a letter to her husband (which will induce a paralytic stroke when he reads it), she confesses guilt for everything but the murder, and promises 'I will encumber you no more.' By which we understand, she will disappear without trace. She veils and dresses for the outside weather; it is winter, and bitterly cold. She 'leaves all her jewels and her money' (although she evidently keeps her watch), and slips out into the early-morning London streets.

It is not at all apparent at this stage what Lady Dedlock's intentions are – but it is clear enough that she has a plan of some kind. As we reconstruct it, her first intention is to go down to St Albans to have a last unseen sight of Esther. She does not intend to speak to her daughter, merely to gaze at her from afar. Why she does not take money sufficient for the train or coach is mysterious. Presumably she thinks that travel on public transport would make her too conspicuous. But, as subsequent events make clear, a well-dressed gentlewoman, walking the winter roads of outer London, is a sight that sticks in observers' minds. The lady is, we deduce, not thinking straight.

For whatever reason, Lady Dedlock resolves to *walk* the twenty-odd miles into Hertfordshire and to Bleak House. When she arrives, many hours later, she discovers that Esther is in fact in London. She evidently gives up hope of having a last sight of her daughter. Lady Dedlock persuades the brick-maker's wife, Jenny, to change clothes with her, and travel on in a northwards direction. This, she hopes, will throw any pursuers off the scent. Jenny's brutish husband is bribed into complicity with the last of Lady Dedlock's valuables, her watch – something that, presumably, she had hoped to give to Esther.

Now dressed less conspicuously in Jenny's clothes, Lady Dedlock retraces her steps, walking back to London. Why, one wonders? Meanwhile, Esther and Bucket are in close pursuit. Conceivably, their paths actually cross on the London–St Albans road: they galloping post-haste north, she limping painfully south on the road that is now the A1. Before leaving London, Bucket has cast a shrewd eye over Lady Dedlock's private apartments. He notes, among other things, that she has taken no money or valuables with her ('rum', he thinks). His first deductions are clear. A woman who does not need money is one who is going on her last journey in life, for which there is no charge – the river, that is. Bucket's first stop is by Lime-house, to check if Lady Dedlock has thrown herself in the Thames, off one of the metropolitan bridges favoured by des-perate females.

Esther observes Bucket make his discreet inquiries of the river warden, whose job it is to scoop the day's harvest of corpses out of the water: 'A man yet dank and muddy, in long swollen sodden boots and a hat like them, was called out of a boat, and whispered with Mr Bucket, who went away with him down some slippery steps – as if to look at something secret that he had to show.' But the woman's corpse which the warden shows Bucket is, evidently, not that of a gentlewoman, or this particular gentlewoman ('thank God').

Bucket and Esther continue their pursuit of Lady Dedlock, by fast private coach, to the edge of St Albans, arriving between five and six in the morning. Lady Dedlock had passed the same way between eight and nine the previous evening. When they arrive at the brickmaker's cottage, Bucket and Esther discover that neither Lady Dedlock nor Jenny is there. The astute Bucket (but not the sweetly unsuspicious Esther) penetrates the 'change of clothes' ruse at once. But for inscrutable reasons of his own, the detective keeps Esther in the dark. (As his notes show, Dickens was in two minds whether to keep the reader in the dark as well, and decided against it.)

Bucket and Esther retrace their steps to London. It is now snowing hard. They arrive back in the capital around four. In Holborn, they pick up Lady Dedlock's trail again at the Snagsby household (Esther still thinks that they are, for reasons she cannot fathom, following Jenny). Woodcourt now joins them. Guster has a letter from Lady Dedlock, which she has been asked to deliver by hand. The girl has also been told to delay any pursuit as best she can. Bucket quickly gets possession of Lady Dedlock's letter, and shakes the truth out of a feebly obstinate Guster.

In her letter Lady Dedlock declares that she has only two objects left in life: 'to elude pursuit, and to be lost'. 'I have no purpose but to die,' she says bleakly. 'Cold, wet, and fatigue, are sufficient causes for my being found dead; *but I shall die of others*, though I suffer from these. It was right that all that had sustained me should give way at once and that I should die of terror and my conscience' (my emphasis).

Guster, under pressure from the remorseless Bucket, reveals that Lady Dedlock has asked directions to 'the poor burying ground . . . where the man was buried that took the sleeping stuff' (i.e. where Hawdon, having committed suicide with an overdose of opium, is buried). One element in Lady Dedlock's plan is now clear; she wishes to be buried as a destitute vagrant alongside her lover. This is why she has taken no money, and disguised herself as a working-class woman. (Although Dickens is too delicate to mention the fact, we have to suppose that she has exchanged her fine silk underclothes with Jenny as well, and discarded her wedding ring and those 'sparkling rings' which so impressed Jo, when she made her earlier visit to the 'berryin' place'.) Her body will be found and, without any identifying marks, deposited without ceremony in a pauper's grave alongside Hawdon's, or so she hopes.

Woodcourt, Bucket and Esther now hurry to the 'berrying place'. There, beneath the 'horrible arch', lies a body. At last Bucket tells Esther the truth ('They changed clothes at the cottage'), but the distracted girl cannot take the information in.

I saw before me, lying on the step, the mother of the dead child [i.e. Jenny]. She lay there, with one arm creeping round a bar of the iron gate, and seeming to embrace it. She lay there, who had so lately spoken to my mother. She lay there, a distressed, unsheltered, senseless creature. She who had brought my mother's letter, who could give me the only clue to where my mother was; she, who was to guide us to rescue and save her whom we had sought so far, who had come to this condition by some means connected with my mother that I could not follow, and might be passing beyond our reach and help at that moment; she lay there, and they stopped me! I saw, but did not comprehend, the solemn and compassionate look in Mr Woodcourt's face. I saw, but did not comprehend, his touching the other on the breast to keep him back. I saw him stand uncovered in the bitter air, with a reverence for something. But my understanding for all this was gone.

I even heard it said between them:

'Shall she go?'

'She had better go. Her hands should be the first to touch her. They have a higher right than ours.'

I passed on to the gate, and stooped down. I lifted the heavy head, put the long dank hair aside, and turned the face. And it was my mother, cold and dead.

Esther falls ill at this point, and we learn nothing of the inquest, nor what verdict is passed on the death of Lady Dedlock.

Schwarzbach's 'smallpox' thesis is beguiling. Lady Dedlock is, as in coroners' terminology, 'a well nourished woman' with no history of invalidism. *Something*, we assume, must have killed her. Those 'filthy stains' are a plausible 'cause of death'. Susan Shatto, in an answering article entitled 'Lady Dedlock and the Plot of *Bleak House*',[3] begs to disagree and gives powerful reasons for her disagreement. While accepting that smallpox infects Jo, Charley, and Esther, she is entirely unconvinced that Lady Dedlock contracts the disease. Nor does she believe that smallpox kills Jo. He finally succumbs to pulmonary tuberculosis, she maintains.

The time-scheme, as Shatto points out, contradicts Schwarzbach's 'fever' hypothesis. There are *two years* intervening between the 'filthy stains' contamination in Chapter 16 and Lady Dedlock's death in Chapter 59. It stretches credulity to imagine that the disease would have remained latent for two years in its host: 'Dickens would surely [have] known the average period of incubation [was] usually ten to twelve days, and at the maximum seventeen days.' It is true that Victorians (as Carlyle's famous description of the infected shirt in *Past and Present* indicates) believed that clothing could harbour disease and spread it to the upper classes. But Lady Dedlock's servant would have been much more at risk than the mistress who, only once, borrowed her clothes – assuming, as is extremely unlikely – she did not wash (and decontaminate) those clothes after Lady Dedlock returned them. There is no intervening source of contagion that we know about.

It is a persuasive refutation. The smallpox hypothesis is attractive, but unsustainable – unless one assumes wilful medical ignorance on Dickens's part, and among his readers. Less persuasive, perhaps, is Shatto's theory of what *does* kill Lady Dedlock: 'Most readers would consider a forty-two-mile journey on foot through a snowstorm sufficient for a cosseted lady suffering great emotional stress to grow pale, exhausted, hoarse, miserable, and ultimately, to die.' If for 'cosseted' one were to read 'well fed', 'most readers' might not wholeheartedly agree. Lady Dedlock is in her mid-forties, or just under fifty (Dickens is delicate about the precise age). We are given no hint that she is an invalid. In fact, the evidence suggests that she is anything but a weakling. She has borne a child in secret and defied conventional morality by none the less making her way in the world with nothing but her looks and will to assist her. This, we deduce, is a tough woman. She is capable of making trips at night in disguise to graveyards in slum areas of London. She evidently knows how to look after herself on the streets. On her last journey to St Albans and back she has had rest, shelter (and some liquid refreshment) at both the brickmaker's cottage and in Holborn.

Lady Dedlock obviously *intends* to die by her lover's grave. This is the script she has written for her last act. But death does not come on time simply because it is dramatically 'right' that it should do so – except in fairy stories and melodrama. There is also the strange business of Bucket's and Woodcourt's reactions when they see the body on the steps. How – from a distance of many yards – do they *know* it is a corpse? Why do they take their hats off? Woodcourt is a medical man. Noble as the gesture is, holding back until Esther has had time to examine the body of her mother ('she has a higher right') would seem to contravene his Hippocratic oath. Unless, that is, he knew that any medical attention is now entirely useless.

If it were merely exhaustion that had felled Lady Dedlock, the doctor's duty (with the detective at his heels) would be to rush forward, elbowing Esther out of the way if necessary, shouting – 'Make way, make way, I'm a medical man.' He would feel her pulse, chafe her wrists, apply restoratives and smelling-salts, burn feathers under her nose. If there were any flicker of life, he would punch her chest, try artificial respiration, wrap her in warm coverings.

And although exhausted (if it were only exhaustion that had rendered her insensible) there would be every expectation that some life might remain in a healthy, forty-year-old woman after a day-and-a-half's exposure and that the prompt attention of a medical man might revive it. Well-fed, warmly clothed, middle-aged people have survived the London streets longer than that – and do so around us every day.

On her part, Esther assumes the body slumped on the steps is 'senseless', not dead. But Bucket evidently knows better. It is too late. There are a string of clues as to how he knows that the body lying in front of them is lifeless, beyond resuscitation. The fact that she stripped herself of money and jewels initially persuaded him that the woman intended to do away with herself, and had a plan for doing so – quickly and efficiently (when did Lady Dedlock ever dither?). Hence Bucket's first stop at the river. Having met a dead end there, Bucket deduced (from the evidence of Esther's handkerchief in Lady Dedlock's jewel-case) that the mother will have gone to take a last glimpse of her child in St Albans (as she thinks). There are further clues for Bucket in Lady Dedlock's statement that 'I shall die' – but not of cold, wet, and fatigue. She has asked directions to where 'the man was buried that took the sleeping stuff' (as Guster gratuitously adds). Dickens, evidently, does not want us to forget that Hawdon took his own life by overdosing on opium (easily acquired by anyone at this period). Someone like Lady Dedlock, given to midnight insomniac walks in London and in Lincolnshire, would certainly have had a supply of opium or laudanum in her medicine cabinet. How does Bucket know, from many yards distant, that Lady Dedlock is dead as a doornail? Because he has (correctly) worked out that she has killed herself.

How? With the desperate woman's best friend, opium.

The balance of probability is, we deduce, not that Lady Dedlock died of delayed smallpox, nor cold and exhaustion, but that, like Hawdon, she poisoned herself. The prospect of being revived, unmasked as the mother of an illegitimate child, publicly tried, and haled off to prison for murder would be too awful. Nor would Lady Dedlock *risk* that happening.

Why then, do Bucket and Woodcourt not say something? Bucket – in the business of Jenny's clothes – has shown an ability to keep facts to himself. There was a particular reason for taciturnity where suicide was concerned. Nineteenth-century regulations as to the interment of those guilty of '*felo de se*' were savagely punitive. Up to 1823 the suicide was required to be buried at a crossroads, in unconsecrated ground, with a stake through the heart (the barbarous ceremony was, for obvious reasons, rarely carried out). Until 1880 the suicide was required to be buried without rites of Christian sepulture. For this reason magistrates, investigating police, and doctors signing death certificates were generously vague, misleading, or simply silent as to cause of death. As, indeed, Woodcourt is when he is called to Hawdon's body. He does *not want to know* if Hawdon took an overdose:

'He has died,' says the surgeon, 'of an over-dose of opium, there is no doubt. The room is strongly flavoured with it. There is enough here now,' taking an old teapot from Mr Krook, 'to kill a dozen people.'

'Do you think he did it on purpose?' asks Krook.

'Took the over-dose?'

'Yes!' Krook almost smacks his lips with the unction of a horrible interest.

'I can't say. I should think it unlikely, as he has been in the habit of taking so much. But nobody can tell.'

Guster is less circumspect.

The suspicion of suicide explains a little exchange between Jo and 'the servant', Lady Dedlock, in which she is particularly inquisitive on the question of whether Hawdon has been buried in consecrated ground:

> The servant [Lady Dedlock] shrinks into a corner – into a corner of that hideous archway, with its deadly stains contaminating her dress; and putting out her two hands, and passionately telling him to keep away from her, for he is loathsome to her, so remains for some moments. Jo stands staring, and is still staring when she re-covers herself.
>
> 'Is this place of abomination, consecrated ground?'
>
> 'I don't know nothink of consequential ground,' says Jo, still staring.
>
> 'Is it blessed?'
>
> 'WHICH?' says Jo, in the last degree amazed.
>
> 'Is it blessed?'
>
> 'I'm blest if I know,' says Jo.

Hawdon, evidently, *does* lie in consecrated ground and had some form of Christian burial, even though he took his own life. Ironically, Lady Dedlock is buried in the Mausoleum in Lincolnshire: separated in death from her lover. But, it is clear, the verdict on her at the coroner's inquest cannot have been suicide. Nor would Bucket, or Woodcourt, say anything to put such a thought in the investigating magistrate's mind.

The death of Lady Dedlock is no minor episode in *Bleak House*. Dickens gives it pride of place as a 'number ending', with a vivid 'curtain line' and one of the novel's forty illustrations. It is a narrative high point. The reader is bound to be curious as to how she dies, and we have – I think – four options. The smallpox hypothesis is attractive, but medically unsound in ways that Dickens would certainly have been aware of. Exhaustion is more likely, but the timing of the death is unsettlingly convenient – more convenient than such deaths are in real life.

This leads to what one might call the 'melodrama' option. In melodrama, heroines can and do die of such non-pathological conditions as 'broken heart' or 'grief' at precisely the right theatrical moment. In life, 'stress' and 'despair' do kill – but usually in undramatic, protracted, messy and untimely ways. The melodramatic option is plausible but not flattering to Dickens's 'art', nor does it fit in a novel which is elsewhere so successfully realistic.

The fourth option is that Lady Dedlock, like Hawdon (whose death she in other ways imitates, as I have suggested), did away with herself by the opium which she would surely have to hand in her medicine-box. (The drug was not even minimally controlled in Britain until the Pharmacy Act of 1868; before then it was more easily available – and cheaper – than beer.) As with Hawdon, the benevolent authorities gloss over the fact of her suicide – Sir Leicester will not know; Esther will not know; the world will not know. The place in Lincolnshire can have its grand funeral. Of the options, I prefer the fourth, although it is unenforceable by clinching evidence.

How Long Is Alice in Wonderland for?

The above is a minor puzzle among those in the most puzzle-packed of Victorian narratives, *Alice's Adventures in Wonderland*. The story opens:

> Alice was beginning to get very tired of sitting by her sister on the bank, and of having nothing to do: once or twice she had peeped into the book her sister was reading, but it had no pictures or conversations in it, 'and what is the use of a book,' thought Alice, 'without pictures or conversations?'
>
> So she was considering, in her own mind (as well as she could, for the hot day made her feel very sleepy and stupid), whether the pleasure of making a daisy-chain would be worth the trouble of getting up and picking the daisies, when suddenly a White Rabbit with pink eyes ran close by her.

It is, we apprehend, gloriously high summer. The 'hot day', the daisies, and the dress in which Tenniel portrays the little girl confirm this seasonal dating. It would be logical to assume the setting in Carroll's mind was 4 July 1862; the day, that is, when Charles Lutwidge Dodgson took Alice Liddell, and her sisters Lorina and Edith, on the boating trip on the Cherwell. On that day, as literary history records, *Alice's Adventures in Wonderland* was conceived as an entertainment by the maths don for his young guests.

The vegetation which Carroll describes and Tenniel pictures confirms the midsummer setting: the 'great thistle' behind which Alice hides from the puppy, or the harebells around the mushroom on which the caterpillar sits. Similarly high-summery are

the open-air 'mad tea-party', and the roses in bloom, about which the Queen of Hearts is so tyrannical. This, one confidently gathers, is a July–August story.

How, then, does one make sense of the end? In her dream Alice is growing embarrassingly during the peremptory trial presided over by the King and Queen of Hearts. Defying the ordinance that 'all persons more than a mile high should leave the court,' she stays on to hear sentence passed:

'Off with her head!' the Queen shouted at the top of her voice. Nobody moved.

'Who cares for *you*?' said Alice, (she had grown to her full size by this time.) 'You're nothing but a pack of cards!'

At this the whole pack rose up into the air, and came flying down upon her; she gave a little scream, half of fright and half of anger, and tried to beat them off, and found herself lying on the bank, with her head in the lap of her sister, who was gently brushing away some dead leaves that had fluttered down from the trees upon her face.

'Wake up, Alice dear!' said her sister. 'Why, what a long sleep you've had!'

After Alice has gone off home, her older sister remains sitting on the bank, thinking about Wonderland. She also foresees 'how this same little sister of hers would, in the after-time, be herself a woman'. How the adult Alice would, at some distant point in time, entertain her own children with her dream of Wonderland, 'and find a pleasure in all their simple joys, remembering her own child-life, and the happy summer days'.

So the story ends, with the phrase 'summer days' that seems so appropriate for all the preceding narrative. All, that is, except for that detail about what it was that woke Alice up: 'some dead leaves that had fluttered down from the trees upon her face.' The leaves of brown, as the song tells us, come fluttering down in September and in the rain.

Alice goes to sleep in midsummer and wakes up in autumn, in the sere and yellow leaf of the year. Her sister's exclamation is apposite: 'Why, what a long sleep you've had!' Rip van Alice, one might think. How can one make sense of this? The most attractive hypothesis is that *Alice* is not just the story of a summer afternoon. It is an allegory of the transitions accompanying puberty: the growing-pains which intervene between a little girl's childhood and her young womanhood. This transition is remarkably rapid in physiological terms: it happens in just a few months. The child grows, as we say, 'overnight' – by which we mean in just a few months. Carroll, it seems, plays with the same kind of metaphorical foreshortening in his story. Alice goes down the rabbit-hole a little girl, and comes out – if not an adult woman – a pubescent girl on the brink of womanhood. How long has she been asleep? A few minutes and an epoch.

Does Dickens Know His Train Signals?

Departing from his normal practice, Dickens offers at the end of the serialised *Our Mutual Friend* a 'Postscript: in lieu of Preface'. This afterword reminds readers of what most of them must have well known – that there almost was no concluding part of the novel. Everything after Chapter 51 was, in a sense, a 'postscript', because thereafter Mr Charles Dickens was living on borrowed time.

Our Mutual Friend was serialised from May 1864 to November 1865. As Dickens recalls:

> On Friday the Ninth [of June] in the present year [1865], Mr and Mrs Boffin (in their manuscript dress of receiving Mr and Mrs Lammle at breakfast) were on the South Eastern Railway with me, in a terribly destructive accident. When I had done what I could to help others, I climbed back into my carriage – nearly turned over a viaduct, and caught aslant upon the turn – to extricate the worthy couple. They were much soiled, but otherwise unhurt . . . I remember with devout thankfulness that I can never be much nearer parting company with my readers for ever than I was then, until these shall be written against my life, the two words with which I have this day closed this book: – THE END.

Dickens gives here a vivid thumbnail account of the terrible Staplehurst accident, in which ten less fortunate passengers perished and forty were seriously injured. The 2.38 train from Folkestone to London (Dickens had been in France) crashed at speed on a viaduct under repair. The system of red-flag warnings (it was daylight) had failed. Dickens's was the only one of seven first-class carriages not to fall off the viaduct. In the above, semi-comic account, Dickens omits to mention his own heroic conduct in aiding the injured and dying. He also omits to mention that, in addition to Mr and Mrs Boffin, his mistress Miss Ellen Ternan and her mother were in the train with him.

The trauma of the Staplehurst accident may well have shortened Dickens's life. It certainly made him nervous about trains. As his son Henry recalled, after Staplehurst, 'I have seen him sometimes in a railway carriage when there was a slight jolt. When that happened he was almost in a state of panic and gripped the seat with both hands.'[1] The Boffin–Lammle breakfast episode Dickens mentions as carrying with him occurs in Book IV, Chapter 2 ('The Golden Dustman Rises a Little').

Oddly enough, there's a railway scene a few chapters earlier in which – as we may think – a terrible rail accident is eerily forecast. It occurs at the end of Book III, Chapter 9. Bella Wilfer and 'the Secretary' (John Rokesmith) have come to Betty Higden's pauper's funeral, near Henley-on-Thames. After her conversation with Lizzie Hexam, in which the two young ladies strike up a friendship, Bella and Rokesmith make their way back to the railway station and the train that will carry them back to London. It is night as they approach the station on foot. From the fact that they can see the signal-lights, they must be coming to the station in the same direction as the train is travelling (i.e. up-line):

> The railway, at this point, knowingly shutting a green eye and opening a red one, they had to run for it. As Bella could not run easily so wrapped up, the Secretary had to help her. When she took her opposite place in the carriage corner, the brightness in her face was so charming to behold, that on her exclaiming, 'What beautiful stars and what a glorious night!' the Secretary said 'Yes,' but seemed to prefer to see the night and the stars in the light of her lovely little countenance, to looking out of [the] window.

O boofer lady, fascinating boofer lady! If I were but legally executor of Johnny's will! If I had but the right to pay your legacy and to take your receipt! – Something to this purpose surely mingled with the blast of the train as it cleared the stations, all knowingly shutting up their green eyes and opening their red ones when they prepared to let the boofer lady pass.

One notes the slight, but palpable, differences in Victorian rail travel from ours. Because they wore bulkier clothes than us (particularly crinolined women) and had a baffling array of carriages to choose from (three 'classes', 'ladies only', 'smoking' – i.e. gentlemen only), simply alighting and descending from the train were complex operations and might take some minutes. To warn passengers, Victorian stations had a 'departure bell' (not to be confused with the whistle, which was a signal for the driver). Dickens specifically mentions this bell, in a later railway scene in *Our Mutual Friend*, where Bradley Headstone has his epileptic fit.

Getting on board was, as I have said, a much more fussy business than it was to become in the twentieth century. And once aboard and settled inside the appropriate carriage, the dim, oil-fuelled lights would allow one to see the stars outside (all modern travellers can see by night are their own reflections – the interior being so much brighter than the exterior). Steam engines give a warning blast as they move off or sound a warning toot from their whistles as they thunder through stations.

But one thing has not changed over the last 130 years: red means 'stop' and green means 'go'. How then, should we understand the description of the signals in the above passage? Victorians, of course, did not have the profusion of highway traffic-lights that we have. They did not have the Highway Code drummed into them as kindergarten pedestrians. It might be that they, in general, had as little sense of railway signalling codes as most present-day sea travellers do of whether red stands for starboard or green for port.

In the above passage, Dickens clearly describes what looks like a dangerously wrong sequence. Modern passengers, seeing a red platform signal-light come on, would assume that there was no need to 'run for it'. The train will only leave when the light turns to green. That is when you would run. No driver will drive his train through a red light. And in Dickens's final sentences, the business of the railway stations 'all knowingly shutting up their green eyes and opening their red ones when they prepared to let the boofer lady pass' would seem to lay the ground for any number of Staplehursts.

Is Bella's beauty so radiant as to have disorientated the signals, so they do not know their red from their green? Is there, perhaps, some play with the symbolism of Othello's 'green-eyed monster' or Macbeth's 'bleeding eye of day' which overrides the signalling codes of the Great Western Railway (which the couple are evidently riding, if they have been to Henley and back)? However ingenious, it is hard to make headway here with the traditional literary associations of red and green.

The most satisfactory explanation of this problem is given by T. S. Lascelles, in his article 'A Railway Signal Puzzle in *Our Mutual Friend*'.[2] Lascelles argues that 'Dickens had seen and correctly observed the old time-interval system of train working.' The explication of how the 'old time-interval system' worked is complicated, but basically as follows. This signalling system was developed before the electric telegraph allowed stations to know that a train was coming, or what other traffic might be on the line. All that the managers of the station knew, for certain, was that a train had arrived when they saw it come in. A technique was thus devised by which, when a train drew in, the green signalling lamp would (by the dropping of a filter over the lens of a bright oil-lamp) turn red. It would remain red for a 'safe' period after the train had departed – say ten minutes. The red signal did not indicate to the driver waiting at the station 'don't go'; it indicated 'We shall ensure no one follows you too closely, so leave at your discretion – but don't wait too long.' The signal-light would not be placed at the head of the platform, but in the middle, where it would be more visible to the majority of passengers and to incoming trains.

What, above all, had to be avoided was an incoming train – particularly a 'through' train – crashing into one which had already halted at the station, or that was still moving slowly out of the station. For this reason the signal-light at the rear end of the station to the oncoming train, the first light the driver would see, needed to be red as well. And it, like the front light, would stay red for some time after the train ahead left. So when Rokesmith and Bella see the red light, this, as Lascelles points out, is no guarantee that the train in the Henley-on-Thames Station is still waiting – it could be just gone, or about to leave. All that it indicates is that a train is in the vicinity. On modern stations, a green light following a red means a train is coming – stand by. When the time-interval system operated, a green light did not mean a train was coming; 'All it could definitely mean was that the previous train had gone by so many minutes.'

The Lascelles explanation, counterfactual as it seems to us and extremely hard to grasp, is satisfying, although not without some difficulties in the application. As Lascelles notes, Dickens was extraordinarily observant. It must have struck him, however, that in the 1860s the time-interval system of signalling was extremely antique. The Great Western Railway began experimenting with electrical-telegraphic signalling techniques in the late 1830s, and they were universal a decade later. As Lascelles notes: 'As electric telegraphy spread, the "time interval" gave place to the "space" interval and what was called . . . the "block system",' which resulted in the signalling conventions we are familiar with today. If, as Dickens noted, *Our Mutual Friend* was set 'in these very times of ours', the time-interval system would have been a thing of the distant past. As Lascelles points out, the line which Bella and John travel on to Henley-on-Thames opened in 1857, with up-to-date telegraphic signalling (of the kind familiar to us). The 'time-interval' system had no place on this line. One can make sense of the red–green signalling paradox only by recourse to a chronological paradox: one of Dickens's many time-warp effects. Bella and John are not only travelling at unimpeded speed, they are travelling thirty years in the past.

What English Novel Is Anna Reading?

If Tolstoy's novel *Anna Karenina* had ended a fifth of the way through, at the end of Chapter 29, we would have a bitter-sweet short story with a happy ending. In this chapter Anna is returning from Moscow to her home, her beloved son Seriozha, and her less than beloved husband, Alexei, in St Petersburg. She has been in the capital to sort out the marriage problems of her hapless sister-in-law, Dolly.

In Moscow, Anna has fallen under the spell of the dashing cavalry officer, Count Vronsky. But she has not surrendered to temptation. She is still a virtuous wife and matron. By no means entirely happy: but virtuous.

She now travels back to St Petersburg by train, at night, accompanied by her maid, Annushka. 'Well, that's all over, thank Heaven!' Anna thinks as she enters her 'dimly lit' carriage: 'Thank Heaven, tomorrow I shall see Seriozha and Alex Alexandrovich again and my good accustomed life will go on as of old':

> With the same preoccupied mind she had had all that day, Anna prepared with pleasure and great deliberation for the journey. With her deft little hands she unlocked her red bag, took out a small pillow which she placed against her knees, and locked the bag again; then she carefully wrapped up her feet and sat down comfortably. An invalid lady was already going to bed. Two other ladies began talking to Anna. One, a fat old woman, while wrapping up her feet, remarked upon the heating of the carriage. Anna said a few words in answer, but not foreseeing anything interesting from the conversation asked her maid to get out her reading-lamp, fixed it to the arm of her seat, and took a

paperknife and an English novel from her handbag. At first she could not read. For a while the bustle of people moving about disturbed her, and when the train had finally started it was impossible not to listen to the noises; then there was the snow, beating against the window on her left, to which it stuck, and the sight of the guard, who passed through the carriage closely wrapped up and covered with snow on one side; also the conversation about the awful snowstorm which was raging outside distracted her attention. And so it went on and on: the same jolting and knocking, the same beating of the snow on the window-pane, the same rapid changes from steaming heat to cold, and back again to heat, the gleam of the same faces through the semi-darkness, and the same voices, – but at last Anna began to read and to follow what she read. Annushka was already dozing, her broad hands, with a hole in one of the gloves, holding the red bag on her lap. Anna read and understood, but it was unpleasant to read, that is to say, to follow the reflection of other people's lives. She was too eager to live herself. When she read how the heroine of the novel nursed a sick man, she wanted to move about the sick-room with noiseless footsteps; when she read of a member of Parliament making a speech, she wished to make that speech; when she read how Lady Mary rode to hounds, teased her sister-in-law, and astonished everybody by her boldness – she wanted to do it herself. But there was nothing to be done, so she forced herself to read, while her little hand played with the smooth paperknife.

The hero of the novel had nearly attained to his English happiness of a baronetcy and an estate, and Anna wanted to go to the estate with him, when she suddenly felt that he must have been ashamed, and that she was ashamed of the same thing, – but what was she ashamed of? 'What am I ashamed of?' she asked herself with indignant surprise. She put down her book, leaned back, and clasped the paperknife tightly in both hands. There was nothing to be ashamed of.

It's a wonderfully evoked scene – familiar to anyone who has travelled through the night by train, yet strange, in many of its physical details, to a non-Russian reader (how should we visualise that movable 'reading-lamp', for example, hung on the arm of Anna's seat?). Vladimir Nabokov, when a lecturer at Cornell University, used to give a whole lecture to his American undergraduates based on this passage. 'Any ass can assimilate the main points of Tolstoy's attitude toward adultery,' Nabokov asserted, 'but in order to enjoy Tolstoy's art the good reader must wish to visualise, for instance, the arrangement of a railway carriage on the Moscow–Petersburg train as it was a hundred years ago.'[1]

The passage is shot through with omens – trains will not be lucky for Anna. But the attention of the English-speaking reader will be particularly drawn to the 'English novel' whose pages Anna is cutting and reading. We are given precise and detailed descriptions of its narrative. What, then, is it? Surely we can identify it by title? A. N. Wilson, in his life of Tolstoy (London, 1988), is in no doubt that Anna has in her hands a novel by Anthony Trollope. Tolstoy wrote *Anna Karenina* between 1873 and 1878, and it is known that during this period he read and admired Trollope's equally massive novel of parliamentary life, *The Prime Minister*. That novel, published in England in June 1876 (although it cannot have been translated into Russian until a few months later), had a momentous influence on *Anna Karenina*. Trollope's narrative climaxes, brilliantly, with the suicide of the villainous Ferdinand Lopez, in front of a speeding train. There are other such deaths in Victorian fiction (notably Carker's in *Dombey and Son*). But it is likely that the climax of Tolstoy's novel – Anna's self-immolation at Nizhny railway station – is directly indebted to *The Prime Minister*.

There is, however, no scene in *The Prime Minister* in which Lopez makes a speech in Parliament. That episode seems to belong to an earlier Trollope novel, *Phineas Finn, the Irish*

Member (1869), whose narrative revolves around the hero's initial failure to make a good maiden speech to the House, and his eventual success in doing so. And the business about Lady Mary riding to hounds and teasing her sister-in-law seems to allude to still another Trollope novel, *Is He Popenjoy?* (1878), where the spirited heroine, Lady Mary Germain (née Gresley), outrages her husband's strait-laced sisters by dancing and hunting. Mary Germain's husband, however, attains his Englishman's idea of happiness not in the form of a 'baronetcy and an estate', but in the unexpected legacy of a marquisate and an estate. Tolstoy's 'baronetcy' seems to be a recollection of Trollope's *The Claverings* (1867), in which the hero, Harry, unexpectedly inherits a baronetcy, an estate (and some of the attendant guilt which Tolstoy mentions) when his distant cousins are drowned sailing. As for the business of the heroine nursing a sick man – that would seem to be an allusion to a quite different novel – Charlotte Yonge's sensational best-seller of 1853, *The Heir of Redclyffe*, in which the baronet hero, Guy, is nursed on his lingering deathbed by his young wife Amy. They are on their honeymoon in Italy and Guy dies an exemplary Christian death.

What, then, is Tolstoy aiming at with this mélange of bits and pieces of English fiction? What the Russian writer is doing, I suggest, is something rather chauvinistic. It was Virginia Woolf who claimed that there was only one 'adult' novel written in Victorian England – *Middlemarch* (a novel that Tolstoy seems not to have read). The mass of English Victorian novels, particularly with their sugar-stick endings and generally optimistic view of life, were essentially *juvenile*, Woolf thought. Henry James made much the same point when he talked, at the end of the century, of the tyranny of the young reader over the adult novelist.

The point that Tolstoy makes is, I think, that Anna is not reading an English novel so much as 'English fiction' – with all its falsities and its childish addiction to 'happiness', particularly happy endings. To paraphrase the famous opening of *Anna Karenina*, all happy novels are alike, so it does not really matter *which* particular English novel the heroine is reading. What Anna is reading, we apprehend, is a generic English novel – a novel that never existed, but which typifies the genre. And to represent the quintessence of English fiction Tolstoy amalgamates a variety of works by that most English of English novelists, Anthony Trollope, the 'Chronicler of Barsetshire', with a dash of Miss Yonge. He, Count Leo Tolstoy, will write a different kind of novel: one that is harder, sadder, more realistic – Russian, in a word. A novel that does not succumb to the debilitating 'English idea'. 'Expect no pernicious "English happiness" in this Russian novel' is the implicit warning.

What English novel, then, is Anna Karenina reading? All of them and none of them.

The Great Gatsby,
and the Chameleon on Wheels

The Great Gatsby is an infuriating novel. One can't, as it were, ever see it straight. That, presumably, is part of the joke of the grotesque billboard, halfway between West Egg and East Egg (i.e. Long Island and the New York Borough of Queens) that presides, quizzically, over the novel's melodrama:

> . . . above the grey land and the spasms of bleak dust which drift endlessly over it, you perceive, after a moment, the eyes of Doctor T. J. Eckleburg. The eyes of Doctor T. J. Eckleburg are blue and gigantic – their retinas are one yard high. They look out of no face, but, instead, from a pair of enormous yellow spectacles which pass over a non-existent nose. Evidently some wild wag of an oculist set them there to fatten his practice in the borough of Queens, and then sank down himself into eternal blindness, or forgot them and moved away. But his eyes, dimmed a little by many paintless days, under sun and rain, brood on over the solemn dumping ground.

Like Eliot's Tiresias in *The Waste Land*, Eckleburg is both blind and all-seeing.

What, though, does the hero look like, facially? It's a blur. Scour the text as you will, you get no answer. The best one can come up with is that he has 'cropped hair'; a hangover, one presumes, from his Major Gatsby military days.

It being the 1920s – when race, racial type, and eugenics were all the rage – the Gatsby face is an important detail. The odious Tom Buchanan, we learn very early on, is a devotee of the book '*The Rise of the Colored Empires* by this man

Goddard' (clearly referring to *The Rising Tide of Color against White World-Supremacy*, by the eugenicist Lothrop Stoddard, published in 1920). Buchanan, the man who snaffled Daisy from Gatsby while the latter was fighting in France, is, of course, as WASP as his ur-Scots name certifies. He believes in what he calls 'Nordic' blood and the urgency of protecting it from the tinted hordes.

Gatsby (with his absurdly English name) is also, superficially, a WASP. His blood is blue. The first account of his background which he supplies Nick Carraway is, as Lady Archer once said of her Gatsbyesque husband's CV, suspiciously 'creative'.

He's from the mid-West, Jay tells Nick – going on to specify 'San Francisco' which is, of course, as far west as you can go without getting very wet. He was educated at Oxford. His family, he says, all died and he came into a lot of money:

'After that I lived like a young rajah in all the capitals of Europe – Paris, Venice, Rome – collecting jewels, chiefly rubies, hunting big game, painting a little, things for myself only, and trying to forget something very sad that had happened to me long ago.'

As Nick sardonically thinks, the Bois de Boulogne does not exactly teem with tigers.

Later, a more accurate CV is divulged, and very bleak it is. The Great Gatsby is, by birth: 'James Gatz of North Dakota . . . His parents were shiftless and unsuccessful farm people.'

What is one to make – genetically – of that Gatsby = Gatz information? From the invaluable website www.ancestry.com one discovers that American families with the surname 'Gatz' were concentrated, as the national 1920 census reports, around Minnesota and Dakota (none, however, were registered in San Francisco). The name, the same website suggests, is most commonly an Americanisation of the Ukrainian and Polish 'Gac'. Not 'Nordic'. Not so by a mile.

But, conceivably, it is not even Slavic. There is lively discussion on the web (google 'Gatz' + 'Jewish' if you're curious) as to whether the hero's birth name is gentile at all, or whether it might more likely be a version of the Jewish 'Getz' (as in the famous tenor saxophone player, Stan Getz). If, as is widely hypothesised, 'Jay' (a common Jewish abbreviation for 'Jacob') is Jewish, it would go a long way to explaining why the bootlegger Meyer Wolfshiem (based, as all the annotated editions inform us, on the historical crook Arnold Rothstein) not merely befriends Gatsby, but actually makes him his heir, enriching the young man beyond the dreams of avarice.

On the extremer fringes of blogosphere, and in some of the wilder academic conferences, it is suggested there may even be African-American blood coursing through the Gatsby veins – which seems to me a speculation too far. The point is, as already mentioned, Fitzgerald never supplies us the facial image against which we can check these racial stereotypes. Look, and you see only a blur.

The Great Gatsby is a novel which runs on gasoline. Without the automobile, the intricate pattern of comings and goings between East and West Egg and the excursions to Manhattan would be impossible. Nor would the final catastrophe happen – the hit-and-run mowing down of Myrtle Wilson. But here, again, the reader must prepare to be bamboozled, though the source of the 'blur' is chromatic rather than physiognomic.

Gatsby has two cars that we know about. One is a chauffeur-driven Rolls-Royce (appropriate for an Anglophile like him). The other vehicle, which figures centrally, is a vast station wagon, which, we gather, he drives himself. This is how the narrator describes it:

He saw me looking with admiration at his car.

'It's pretty, isn't it, old sport?' He jumped off to give me a better view. 'Haven't you ever seen it before?'

I'd seen it. Everybody had seen it. It was a rich cream colour, bright with nickel, swollen here and there in its monstrous length with triumphant hat-boxes and supper-boxes and tool-boxes, and terraced with a labyrinth of windshields that mirrored a dozen suns. Sitting down behind many layers of glass in a sort of green leather conservatory, we started to town.

The last, violent, episode of *The Great Gatsby* depends on an intricate game of musical chairs (or driving seats). 'Let's all go to town!' suggests Daisy, impulsively. She craves 'fun'. Idle and bored and tense with the coming marital crisis as the company is, the assembled Buchanans, Carraway, and Gatsby drive, in convoy, from East Egg to New York. A flask of (bootleg) whisky goes with them. It is a sunny day.

'Shall we all go in my car?' suggests Jay, feeling 'the hot, green leather of the seat'. It is, of course, vast enough to accommodate them all – and another half-dozen with them if they wanted. 'Is it standard shift?' asks Tom (at that time, cars might well have two sets of gears). On being assured it is standard, he suggests that Jay drives his (Tom's) blue coupé (with Daisy) while he and Nick take the Gatsby-mobile.

Jay is not keen about this arrangement. Nor are Tom's motives for suggesting the switch clear. Halfway to town, under the myopic stare of Eckleburg's ominous eyes, Buchanan stops at George Wilson's service station: ostensibly for gas. There may be another motive. Myrtle Wilson is Tom's mistress.

The suspicious husband (who is not aware who exactly is cuckolding him) has locked Myrtle in the house. What, Tom asks Wilson, does he think of the car he is driving? adding 'I bought it last week.' As he turns the gas pump handle, Wilson replies, non-committally, 'It's a nice yellow one.' Why does Tom lie about ownership of the 'yellow' (no longer 'cream') car? Is it to throw Wilson off the track?

In the suite they take at the Plaza Hotel, by Central Park, a terrible scene ensues, over who shall have Daisy. It ends with her saying she can't stand it any more. They leave, again in convoy. She and Jay return to Long Island – now (another musical-chair switch) – in his car. Tom and Nick will return in the Buchanan blue coupé.

It is 'cooling twilight'. Myrtle Wilson finally escapes from the room in which George has imprisoned her and 'rushed out into the dusk'. She is hit by a car, and killed. The car does not stop. Michaelis, who runs the nearby coffee joint, witnesses the accident but 'wasn't even sure of [the car's] colour – he told the first policeman that it was light green'. The car was going, he hazards, 'thirty or forty miles an hour'.

He is not the sole witness. A 'pale well-dressed negro', who was driving in the on-coming direction and also saw the accident, corrects Michaelis. The 'death car' was 'going fifty, sixty', he calculates. And, as to colour, it was a 'big yellow car'. It was, of course, Gatsby's vehicle. Later, he confides to Carraway that Daisy was driving, 'but of course I'll say I was. You see, when we left New York she was very nervous and she thought it would steady her to drive.'

It's not the nerve tonic that most doctors would prescribe. Is Jay – inveterate liar – telling the truth? Even at dusk, surely one of the witnesses would have observed the driver was a woman not a man? Particularly at thirty miles an hour. Whatever, by taking the rap Gatsby has signed his death-warrant at the hands (and gun) of the vengeful Wilson.

So: is the 'death car' cream, light green, or yellow? What is it, a chameleon on wheels? The detail about the green leather upholstery (it, at least, stays the same colour) confirms that it is the same car, not the Rolls-Royce, which is in question here. But the confusion over colour (colour being an element which is hugely significant in the design of the narrative) cannot be accidental. *The Great Gatsby* was proof-read by the greatest, and most meticulous, editor in the history of literature:

Maxwell Perkins. The chromatic blur is, without question, an artistically motivated and intentional device on the author's part. It is there for a reason. But what is that reason?

Partly, I suspect, it is there to create in the reader the impression that nothing is what it seems. Gatz/Gatsby, cream cars/yellow cars, bootleggers/Oxonians. Like Michaelis and the pale negro (an odd oxymoron) the reader does not read the novel as one might a legal document. *The Great Gatsby* is viewed through the prism of its language. And viewed with the chronic imperfection of the human eye. Or the Eckleburg eye.

Brideshead: The Tradesman's Entrance

One of the interesting things about novels with good stories is that they often have other good stories nestled behind them – unnarrated, but none the less *there*; radiating mistily and tantalisingly.

Brideshead Revisited has an impressive cluster. It's a novel, for example, whose central landscape and portraiture (the narrator is an artist) has a precisely delineated World War II frame. Charles Ryder and the two heads of the Marchmain family (the Marquess and his eldest son, 'Bridey') serve in war. But only one character that we know of in the novel actually wins a medal for wartime heroism. Who?

It's Cordelia, the charmingly saucy young convent girl who, alas, grows up into a 'quite plain' and excessively grave spinster. In 1936 Cordelia went off to Spain to drive an ambulance where the guns were firing. After the war, as she reports: 'the authorities were very polite, thanked me for all I'd done, gave me a medal, and sent me packing.'

It is, of course, Franco's Rebels – the Nationalists, the Fascists – for whom Cordelia was driving and saving lives. It's nice to think that she might have blundered into Miss Brodie's disciple, Joyce Emily, in the mêlée. Muriel Spark's heroine, we recall, is a fanatic fascista. Were the Marchmain-Flytes passive sympathisers with the *Caudillo*, the *Duce* and the *Führer* in the 1930s? What was Lord Marchmain's attitude to the Italian dictator, while he was resident in Venice? Grateful that someone, at last, had made the gondolas run on time?

At the end of the narrative, in 1943, we deduce from Nanny Hawkins's amiably senile ramblings that both Cordelia and Julia are now in Palestine – nursing, perhaps, or otherwise giving comfort to the British forces. Women, it would seem, see much more action than the men in this novel, whose plot interweaves, inextricably, with world war.

The most interesting nurse, doing her good works in the novel's narrative hinterland, is Charles's mother. She merits no more than a sentence in the story (Sebastian's mother, by contrast, gets whole chapters – she is, of course, a Marchmain). On his first visit to Brideshead, challenged to offer something about *his* background, Charles ventures to Sebastian (odd he hasn't enquired earlier) the tightest-lipped of family histories:

> 'There is only my father and myself. An aunt kept an eye on me for a time but my father drove her abroad. My mother was killed in the war.' ['Oh . . . how very unusual,' interjects Sebastian in what is evidently a momentary silence.]
>
> 'She went to Serbia with the Red Cross. My father has been rather odd in the head ever since. He just lives alone in London with no friends and footles about collecting things.'

It is, one perceives, the tight-lip of embarrassment: the *mauvaise honte* of the inveterate snob, who knows that his card in life has been invincibly overtrumped. The Ryders are social nothings, with the towers of Brideshead looming over them. The nothingness, we suspect, rather irks Charles.

Born around 1903, like Waugh himself, Charles must have known his mother, before she went off to die so strangely and so gallantly. World War I began in Serbia and ended with the establishment of its precarious modern state. Waugh, himself, fought in Croatia, in World War II, which may be where Charles is eventually headed. Who knows, he may even take time off to put flowers on his mother's grave.

Serbia was the site of some heroic British nursing in World War I. The following is the account of one such lady with a lamp, which I have lifted, at random, from the web. Flora Sandes was conceivably (if we allow fancy free rein) a comrade of Nurse Ryder's. Perhaps, like Sandes, Charles's mother swapped 'bandages for guns', and thereby fell in battle, not to some wayward shell, or wretched disease:

> By 12 August 1914, the Englishwoman Flora Sandes knew that if she wanted an exciting life, she would have to fight for it. That was the date she steamed out of London, along with 36 other eager nurses, bound for Serbia. Within 18 months, during the great retreat to Albania, she had exchanged bandages for guns. She insisted on acting as a soldier, and being treated as such; therefore, like male combatants, she cared for the wounded, but only 'between shots'. She curtly informed one correspondent on 10 November 1916 that if people thought she ought to be a nurse instead of a soldier, they should be told that 'we have Red Cross men for first aid'. Her martial valour during World War I was recognised in June 1919 when a special Serbian Act of Parliament made her the first woman to be commissioned in the Serbian Army.

Alas, Mrs Ryder did not survive for such official honour. Nor is she much mentioned or commemorated, one gathers, among her family. The sentence Charles throws Sebastian's way is all Nurse Ryder gets by way of memorial.

The reader finds it hard to leave it there. Why, one may ask, did this woman take off for Serbia in the first place? Not patriotism. There were few British soldiers' lives at risk in that theatre, unlike France. What motives can have driven her to abandon her wifely and motherly duties? Sandes, like the vast majority of female nurses and ambulance drivers, was a fiercely single woman. (As Radclyffe Hall's *The Well of Loneliness* confirms, many lesbians found a role in the man's world via the Red Cross in wartime.) Is Charles telling the whole truth? Was there some family crisis?

Charles's father, we are told, is in his 'late fifties' in 1922. And, as his son notes, it pleases him to act decades older. Presumably he was similarly superannuated by birth-date and demeanour during the war years. Too old to serve and disinclined to lie about his age to the recruiting sergeant, as other gallant fifty-year-olds did. Was his wife, Charles's mother, considerably younger than her spouse? Could that have been a factor in her doomed flight to the Balkans?

Since his wife's death, Ryder Sr has been comically dotty and genteelly misanthropic – interested only in such things as Etruscan funerary customs. The only other salient fact readers glean about his life (among the superfluity of *Biographia Bridesheadiana*) is that he once failed to get a fellowship at All Souls. That too contributed to the dottiness. He thereafter devotes his life to quaintly obsolete antiquarian scholarship. Antique as he is, he is a younger son – there being vague reference to an elder brother. A pompous cousin, Jasper Ryder, appears at Oxford to vex Charles with unwanted good advice. A maiden aunt briefly supplied maternal services, after the Serbian tragedy. She was resented. We never learn the source of Mr Ryder's evidently ample wealth. There was clearly enough to go round – for one inheriting generation at least. His only significant human connection, it would seem, is a son who, in a kind of reverse Oedipalism, he is desperate to get rid of, so that he may the better enjoy his dusty solitude.

Charles's father drifts entirely out of visibility in the later stages of the novel. When does he die? Is it around his son's thirty-ninth year (when Waugh's father died)? That might be a clue to some other untold stories in the novel. Ryder, as every commentator on *Brideshead Revisited* notes, has strong elements of Evelyn Waugh in him. One of the more astute of those commentators, Humphrey Carpenter, notes that Mr Ryder was 'the sort of parent [Evelyn Waugh] was no doubt hoping to be.'

Waugh would, one guesses, not particularly want to be the kind of parent his own father was. Too un-Brideshead by miles. The novelist was sensitive, verging on hypersensitive, about his class origins. His childhood was spent in a respectable, but wholly unprepossessing, family house in Golders Green. The novelist Dan Jacobson once suggested to me that it ought to be the only blue plaque in London with an exclamation mark after it. According to Christopher Hollis, the young Evelyn would take letters to nearby Hampstead, that they might have the classier postmark. He certainly (as paterfamilias of Combe Florey) re-postmarked himself very effectively in later life.

Waugh's father was, horrible to say, a tradesman. Admittedly, it was the book trade. Arthur Waugh was managing director of the venerable Victorian publishing house (Dickens's publishers, no less) Chapman and Hall, from 1902 to 1930. They were, alas, its declining years (as Arthur Waugh's own house-history of Chapman and Hall chronicles). Evelyn's father died in 1943 – the year in which *Brideshead Revisited*'s narrative opens. His father's death, one is told, represented a significant moment of psychic release for the novelist.

In an uncharacteristic outburst to the underbred Lt. Hooper (whose father, doubtless, may have been a tradesman even lower in the social scale than publishing) Ryder indulges in some extravagant self-dramatisation. The younger officer has made the injudiciously fatuous comment that the magnificent pile in which they are to billet themselves was clearly not erected to serve as transit accommodation for a second-rate infantry regiment:

> 'No,' I said, 'not what it was built for. Perhaps that's one of the pleasures of building, like having a son, wondering how he'll grow up. I don't know; I never built anything, and I forfeited the right to watch my son grow up. I'm homeless, childless, middle-aged, loveless, Hooper.'

In terms of what would be considered normal human intercourse, it's an odd description: particularly the self-pitying 'childless'. By his dissolved marriage, Ryder actually has two children, in whom, however, he seems even less interested than his father was in infant Charles. Indeed, Charles could not be bothered, on his return from two years' daubing in the tropics, to meet his children – so excited was he with his adulterous reunion with Julia. Ryder, one gathers (like father like son) *wants* to be rid of the burden of parentage, so that he may glory in the unloved, unloving condition he bemoans to Hooper.

The most perplexing untold story behind the big story of the novel is, like the life history of the hero's mother, thrown off, parenthetically, in a single sentence. Its background is the dark, wholly impenetrable, four-year stretch of narrative from the theatrical death of Lord Marchmain, at Brideshead, to Captain Ryder, commander of C Company, 'revisiting' the house now that it has been requisitioned for wartime use. He is (as was once promised by marriage) its final proprietor. Such are the wretched ironies of twentieth-century history.

Of what has happened in this unnarrated four years we know absolutely nothing – other than that Charles (although over-age) volunteered for the military and broke off all relations with the Brideshead family. We know nothing, that is, except for one tantalising detail.

Having done his 'recce' of the vandalised property, Charles goes to the 'one part of the house I had not yet visited':

> The chapel showed no ill-effects of its long neglect; the art-nouveau paint was as fresh and bright as ever; the art-nouveau lamp burned once more before the altar. I said a prayer, an ancient, newly-learned form of words, and left.

That one sentence about ancient prayers, 'newly-learned', is the only clue that something momentous has happened. Charles has 'gone over'. The precipitating event, the lingering death of the convert, Lord Marchmain, was described in huge detail. What happened thereafter we must reconstruct, or hypothesise, from the scrap given, parenthetically, here.

One thing is certain. After that lordly death, Charles has seen nothing of Julia or any other member of the family since those deadly words: 'I can't marry you, Charles; I can't be with you ever again.' But what interpretation should we put on 'newly-learned'? Surely 'newly' cannot mean some years ago? At the same moment, that is, when he and Julia were for ever cast asunder. Admittedly, Catholic instruction takes time (as Rex Mottram was vexed to discover). But a few months should do it. Did Charles make the decision to convert at the same time as he decided – over-age as he was – to volunteer for the army? Throwing, as it were, a pair of dice into the unknown future?

Was it Hitler who gave Charles this momentous push? Or did he, at some point, become possessed of the idea that Lord Marchmain's final, irresistible, sign of the cross was a miracle, aimed by the Almighty, with the specific aim of bringing him, Charles Ryder, to the true faith? Do his more-than-Trappist complaints to Hooper imply that he intends to go a step further, once demobilised? Is he, like Sebastian, a monk *manqué*? Is his rough serge battledress blouse a preparatory hair shirt?

We shall never know. Waugh left the novel empty at this, most important, juncture. It is, none the less, a tantalisingly echoing emptiness, into which readers are forever tempted to shout their speculations, and listen hopefully for what returns.

*All the books featured in these essays are
published by The Folio Society.*

· NOTES ·

THE SECRET AGENT

1. Norman Sherry, *Conrad's Western World* (London, 1971).
2. Quoted in Arthur Marshall, *Explosives* (London, 1917), II, p. 342.
3. See Frederick Forsyth, *The Fourth Protocol* (London, 1984).

ULYSSES

1. Hugh Kenner, 'Molly's Masterstroke', *James Joyce Quarterly* (Fall 1972), repr. *Ulysses: Fifty Years of Criticism*, ed. Thomas F. Staley (Indiana, 1974), pp. 19–28.
2. Margaret Honton, 'Molly's Mistressstroke', *James Joyce Quarterly* (Fall 1976), pp. 25–6.

THE BIG SLEEP

1. Tom Hiney, *Raymond Chandler: a Biography* (London, 1997), p. 163. Other biographies have the less dramatic reply, 'I don't know.'

REBECCA

1. See Hitchcock, in *Hitchcock* by F. Truffaut with the collaboration of H. G. Scott (New York, 1967), p. 178:

> 'Of course, there's a terrible flaw in the story which our friends, the plausibles, never picked up. On the night when the boat with Rebecca's body in it is found, a rather unlikely coincidence is revealed: on the very evening she is supposed to have drowned, another woman's body is picked up two miles down the beach. And this enables the hero to identify that second body as his wife's. Why wasn't there an inquest at the time the unknown woman's body was discovered?'

Hitchcock cut du Maurier's 'two months' to the same day; but the 'flaw' pre-exists in the novel.

EMMA

1. These essays of Scott's are conveniently collected in Ioan Williams (ed.), *Sir Walter Scott on Novelists and Fiction* (London, 1968).
2. See Edgar Johnson, *Sir Walter Scott: The Great Unknown*, 2 vols (London, 1970), II, p. 1084.
3. R. W. Chapman (ed.), *Emma* (London, 1933), p. 493.

OLIVER TWIST

1. Bayley's essay, 'Things as they are', is to be found in John Gross and Gabriel Pearson (eds), *Dickens and the Twentieth Century* (London, 1962), pp. 49–64.
2. J. Hillis Miller, *Dickens: The World of His Novels* (Cambridge: Mass., 1958).
3. Colin Williamson, 'Two Missing Links in *Oliver Twist*', *Nineteenth-Century Fiction*, 22 (Dec. 1967), pp. 225–34.
4. See Alison Winter, 'Mesmerism and Popular Culture in early Victorian England', *History of Science*, 32 (1994), pp. 317–43. Kaplan discusses the O'Key connection at length in *Dickens and Mesmerism*, pp. 34–44.
5. Kathleen Tillotson (ed.), *Oliver Twist* (Oxford, 1966), p. 392.
6. That Dickens altered his plan of *Oliver Twist* as he went along is convincingly argued by Burton M. Wheeler, 'The Text and Plan of *Oliver Twist*', *Dickens Studies Annual*, 12 (1983), pp. 41–61. Wheeler notes particularly that 'the conspiracy between Monks and Fagin does not bear close scrutiny' (p. 56) and that this section of the novel bears witness of being improvised from one instalment to the next.
7. See *The Letters of Charles Dickens*, vol. 1, 1820–39, ed. Madeline House and Graham Storey (Oxford, 1965), pp. 403, 461.

WUTHERING HEIGHTS

1. Heathcliff's complicated legal manoeuvre is explained in Appendix VI, 'Land Law and Inheritance', by E. F. J. Tucker, in *Wuthering Heights*, ed. Hilda Marsden and Ian Jack (Oxford, 1976), pp. 497–9. Tucker assumes there may have been some 'dishonesty' and collusion between Heathcliff and Mr Green, the Gimmerton attorney, in alienating Hindley so entirely from his inheritance. As Tucker points out, Green evidently 'misinforms' Edgar Linton as to the state of the law, so as to favour Heathcliff's claims. Bribery is implied.

VILLETTE

1. Carol Hanbury Mackay (ed.), *The Two Thackerays: Anne Thackeray Ritchie's Centenary Biographical Introductions to the Works of William Makepeace Thackeray*, 2 vols (New York, 1988), I, p. 385.
2. Guinevere Griest, *Mudie's Circulating Library and the Victorian Novel* (Bloomington: Indiana, 1970), I, p. 21.

THE WOMAN IN WHITE

1. Kenneth Robinson, *Wilkie Collins: A Biography* (London, 1951), p. 149.
2. Nuel P. Davis, *The Life of Wilkie Collins* (Urbana: Illinois, 1956), p. 216.
3. The review is reprinted in Norman Page (ed.), *Wilkie Collins: The Critical Heritage* (London, 1974), pp. 102–3.
4. Ibid., p. 124.
5. Ibid., p. 95.
6. This anomaly in the novel's chronology is noted by W. M. Kendrick, 'The Sensationalism of *The Woman in White*', *Nineteenth-Century Fiction*, 32: 1 (June 1977), pp. 18–35 (see particularly p. 23) and by Andrew Gasson, '*The Woman in White*: A Chronological Study', *Wilkie Collins Society Journal*, 2 (1982), pp. 12–13.

7. J. G. Millais, *The Life and Letters of John Everett Millais* (London, 1899), pp. 278–9.

MIDDLEMARCH

1. *Middlemarch*, ed. R. D. Ashton (Harmondsworth, 1994), p. xxi.
2. R. D. Ashton, *G. H. Lewes* (Oxford, 1990), pp. 10–11.

TESS OF THE D'URBERVILLES

1. See *Thomas Hardy: The Critical Heritage*, ed. R. G. Cox (London, 1970), pp. 217–18.
2. Ibid., p. 212.
3. Tony Tanner, 'Colour and Movement in *Tess of the d'Urbervilles*', *Critical Quarterly*, 10 (Autumn 1968); repr. in R. P. Draper (ed.), *Hardy: The Tragic Novels* (London, 1975), pp. 182–208. The passage quoted comes on p. 205.
4. *The 1890s*, ed. G. A. Cevasco (New York, 1993).
5. Ian Gregor, *The Great Web* (London, 1974), p. 182.
6. *Tess of the d'Urbervilles*, ed. James Gibson (London, 1994), p. 411.
7. Ibid., p. 417.

THE INVISIBLE MAN

1. Harris Wilson, *Arnold Bennett and H. G. Wells: A Record* (Urbana: Illinois, 1960), pp. 34–5.
2. This point is made by Jack Williamson, in *H. G. Wells, Critic of Progress* (Baltimore, 1973), pp. 85–6.

JANE EYRE

1. See Sherrill E. Grace, 'Courting Bluebeard with Bartok, Atwood, and Fowles: Modern Treatment of the Bluebeard Theme', *The Journal of Modern Literature*, 11: 2 (July 1984), pp. 245–62.
2. See, for example, the allusions to Byron's *The Corsair* (1814) by the Ingram party.

THE GOOD SOLDIER

1. Eugene Goodheart, 'What Dowell knew: A Reading of *The Good Soldier*', *Antaeus*, 56 (Spring 1986), p. 70.
2. Martin Stannard (ed.), *The Good Soldier* (Norton Critical Edition, New York, 1991), p. xi.
3. Vincent Cheng, 'A Chronology of *The Good Soldier*', *ELN* 24 (Sept. 1986), repr. in Stannard, p. 385.
4. J. F. Kermode, 'Novels: Recognition and Deception', *Critical Inquiry*, 1: 1 (Sept. 1974), repr. in Stannard, p. 336.
5. Max Saunders, *Ford Madox Ford* (Oxford, 1996), 1, p. 422.

RUTH

1. Mrs Twinn, who has thought deeply about this question, perceives a radical confusion in the author's conception of the 'absent' London episode: 'In Gaskell's mind Ruth and Bellingham did not travel to London at all. However, in the novel, they went to London; (a) because as you rightly comment it would have been the natural route from East Anglia. Close study of the Betts map of 1838 demonstrates that it might have been possible to find a cross-country route but unlikely because of the state of the roads – Bellingham's carriage would have required the better turnpike roads which would have taken them to London; (b) because London provided the right image for Ruth's "deflowering". I believe Gaskell's perception of London was associated with the image of "Babylon". Also Bellingham probably rented a house in London, as was usual amongst the gentry of the time, although I agree he would have been unlikely to have taken Ruth there. I think the choice of London would have been an appropriate and recognisable signal to readers of the events which took place there.' I find Mrs Twinn's reconstruction very persuasive.

BLEAK HOUSE

1. See F. S. Schwarzbach, 'The Fever of *Bleak House*', *English Language Notes*, 20 (Mar.–June 1983), pp. 21–7.
2. F. S. Schwarzbach, ' "Deadly Stains": Lady Dedlock's Death', *Dickens Quarterly*, 4 (Sept. 1987), pp. 160–5.
3. Susan Shatto, 'Lady Dedlock and the Plot of *Bleak House*', *Dickens Quarterly*, 5 (Dec. 1988), pp. 185–91.

OUR MUTUAL FRIEND

1. Peter Ackroyd, *Dickens* (London, 1990), p. 963.
2. T. S. Lascelles, 'A Railway Signal Puzzle in *Our Mutual Friend*', *The Dickensian*, 45 (1949), pp. 213–16.

ANNA KARENINA

1. Brian Boyd, *Vladimir Nabokov: The American Years* (Princeton, 1991), p. 175.